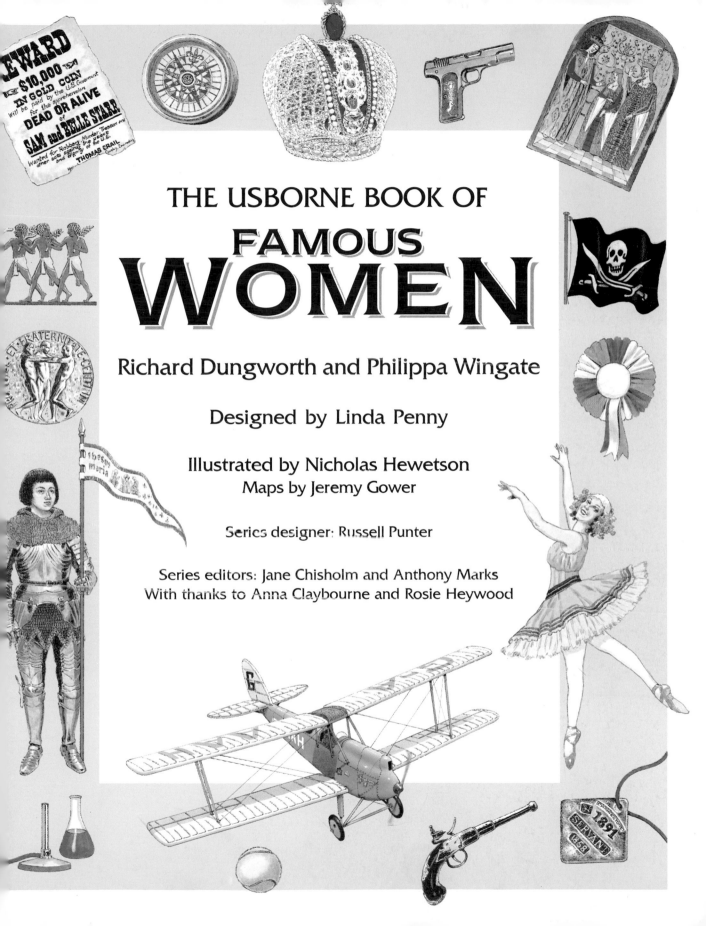

THE USBORNE BOOK OF
FAMOUS
WOMEN

Richard Dungworth and Philippa Wingate

Designed by Linda Penny

Illustrated by Nicholas Hewetson
Maps by Jeremy Gower

Series designer: Russell Punter

Series editors: Jane Chisholm and Anthony Marks
With thanks to Anna Claybourne and Rosie Heywood

CONTENTS

INTRODUCTION

Throughout history, remarkable women have become political leaders, record breakers and world-famous performers. Whether they were responsible for scientific breakthroughs or prison break-outs, these women achieved fame and recognition. This book tells their stories.

Women and fame

Although women can be famous for all kinds of things, they are more likely to be well-known in certain fields. There are many famous female film stars and singers, for example, but fewer famous women politicians, doctors or artists.

Women who reach the top, like tennis champion Steffi Graf, are often paid less than male champions.

Some women, like the British politician Margaret Thatcher, are recognized for having succeeded in a man's world, doing a job traditionally associated with men.

It has always been hard for women to achieve success. This was especially true in the past. Women were traditionally expected to stay at home to bring up children and do housework.

This didn't leave them much time or opportunity to become great artists or athletes.

In many societies, women were "owned" or controlled by husbands, fathers or brothers. They didn't have their own money, which made it very difficult to start a business, travel, or create works of art.

Often the women who did succeed in their chosen field were born into well-off families. This gave them greater freedom from domestic chores to pursue their ambitions.

A 19th-century picture, showing a woman busy at her housework.

A few women chose to disguise themselves as men to escape the traditional female role and gain an education or social freedom. Miranda Stewart (see page 22), for example, spent her life dressed as a man so that she could be a doctor, at a time when women weren't allowed to study medicine.

The spread of fame

In the past, few individuals achieved long-lasting or widespread fame. Today, with mass media such as radio, television and the Internet, news travels across the world in seconds. This means that more women are enjoying greater fame than ever before.

Television creates its own "stars".

Women's rights

In many cultures, women still do not have equal rights. In parts of the world, such as Saudi Arabia and Kuwait, only men can vote. Even in the West, attitudes toward women's rights have changed slowly. In Switzerland, for example, women didn't have a vote until as recently as 1971. Many areas, such as politics, science and learning, are still dominated by men.

Toward the future

The 20th century has seen the growth of the feminist movement, whose followers believe in the social, economic and political equality of women. Women have fought to have the same rights as men and, as a result, things have changed. In many countries, women are allowed to work and have their own money. It is often illegal to discriminate against women in education or employment.

More and more women are rising to the top of their professions. The opportunity for women to gain fame and fortune is growing.

Today, a woman doctor is not an unusual sight.

THE FIRST GREAT WOMEN LEADERS

Since ancient times, there have been exceptional women who, despite the odds against them, have become great rulers. Their power and political skills made them great leaders.

Seizing the throne

Probably the first woman to wield real political power in ancient times was Queen Hatshepsut of Egypt (c.1503-1482BC). She began her career by acting as ruler for her young stepson. But instead of handing over power to him, she seized the throne herself during a religious ceremony.

The priests carried a statue of a god past Hatshepsut. It was so heavy that they sank to their knees.

Hatshepsut said that this was a sign that the gods wanted her to rule. She declared herself "king" of Egypt.

As ruler, she led successful military campaigns in Nubia and Syria, always dressing for battle in men's clothes.

When Hatshepsut died, her stepson finally became pharaoh. He hated Hatshepsut for depriving him of his position, and destroyed all the statues that had been made of her. Archeologists have only recently begun piecing together fragments of stone and finding out more about her achievements. It seems that her reign was very successful. As well as fighting battles, she encouraged trade and exploration, and built great works of architecture.

Nefertiti

Queen Nefertiti (14th century BC) had such a powerful influence over her husband, Akhenaten, that she may have become joint ruler of Egypt.

A stone bust of Nefertiti

Akhenaten showed his love and respect for Nefertiti by giving her a second name, which was Neferneruaten. Usually, only kings were allowed to have two names.

In the 14th year of his reign, Akhenaten declared that someone called Smenkhkare was to become his co-ruler. The pharaoh gave his new co-ruler Nefertiti's name, Neferneruaten.

Very little is known about Smenkhkare. Some historians think the mysterious co-ruler was actually Nefertiti herself. They think Akhenaten believed that his wife would never give birth to a son and heir, so he married his eldest daughter instead. In order to compensate Nefertiti for marrying someone else, he may have made her a "king".

A courageous empress

Theodora (c.497-548) rose from a poor background to become the co-ruler of a vast empire. She was born in Constantinople (now called Istanbul), where her father worked in a circus, taming bears. Theodora, who was famous for her beauty, worked as a dancer and mime artist. Later, she turned to religion and educated herself. While working as a wool spinner, she met Justinian, her future husband.

The palace of the Empress Theodora and Emperor Justinian in Constantinople

The Emperor and Empress were joint rulers and so each had a throne.

We know what kind of clothes were worn at the palace from a church mosaic.

These men have come to arrange a trading agreement.

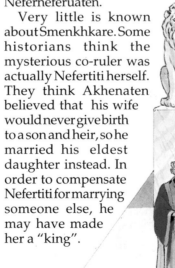

Justinian was the nephew of the Emperor of the Eastern Roman Empire. He fell madly in love with Theodora and married her. In 527, they were crowned Emperor and Empress. They ruled the Empire from their beautiful palace in Constantinople.

Theodora had a great influence on her husband's policies and actions. She used her power to help women and the poor, and Justinian listened closely to her advice.

In 532, riots broke out in the city. Justinian prepared to flee the palace to save his life, but Theodora persuaded him to stay and fight. This proved to be wise advice. Justinian defeated the rioters and he and Theodora stayed in the palace. He survived to rule for over thirty years.

Armed guards protected the palace from attack.

Uniting force

During the 15th century, Queen Isabella (1451-1504) ruled Castile, one of the kingdoms which made up the country now known as Spain. She was a very ambitious queen. Her aim was to unite all the kingdoms and rule over them herself.

Queen Isabella and King Ferdinand

Isabella's first step towards this goal was in 1469, when she married Ferdinand, the heir to Aragon, another of the kingdoms.

The final kingdom to conquer was Granada in the south of Spain. Since the 8th century, it had been occupied by the Moors who were Muslims from north west Africa. Isabella led an army against the Moors herself, and managed to drive them out of Spain. She also forcibly expelled all the Jews who lived in an area of southern Spain called Andalusia. By 1492, Isabella had succeeded in uniting Spain under her control.

During her reign, Isabella extended her empire overseas too. She gave Christopher Columbus, a Portuguese explorer, the money he needed to fund three ships to sail west in search of the Far East. In fact, Columbus ended up in the Bahamas, off the coast of America, by mistake. He became the first European to set foot there.

Columbus' route from Europe to America is shown in blue. His intended route is shown in red.

Columbus's ship, the *Santa Maria*

A great Czarina

A German princess named Princess Sophia of Anhalt-Zerbst (1729-96) married Grand Duke Peter, heir to the Russian throne, when she was 16 years old. She changed her name to Catherine and converted to Russian Orthodoxy, the official religion in Russia.

The marriage was not a happy one. Peter was mentally and physically weak. He spent much of his time playing with toy soldiers. When he became Czar in 1762, Catherine controlled the country. After only six months, she led an uprising and forced Peter off the throne. He later died in prison.

A portrait of Catherine the Great

Catherine ruled Russia for 34 years until her death. During her reign, she encouraged education, art, science and religious tolerance. Although she sympathized with the plight of the poor, she did very little to help them. She ruled the country with a firm hand, putting down any rebellions mercilessly.

Her strength meant that her policies abroad were very successful. During her reign, she expanded Russia's territory, taking land from both Poland and Turkey.

MODERN LEADERS

During the first half of the 20th century, the efforts of women's rights campaigners, and the important role of women in both World Wars, has improved the political status of women in many societies. Some have even been chosen to lead their countries.

Golda Meir

Golda Meir (1898-1978) was born in Kiev, Russia, in a part of the city where Jewish families were forced to live. When she was eight years old, her family emigrated to the United States of America.

Golda trained as a teacher, but became active in Zionism, a political movement that wanted a homeland for Jews in Palestine. After she married, she went to live in Palestine.

She joined the Labour party and took part in creating the independent state of Israel in 1948.

The Israeli flag

Golda Meir held posts of increasing responsibility in the *Knesset*, the Israeli parliament. In 1969, when the Israeli prime minister Eshkol died, Golda took his place. During her five years in power, she campaigned for peace in the Middle East and security for Jews.

In 1973, a crisis known as the Yom Kippur War broke out against Egypt and Syria. Golda Meir helped to negotiate a ceasefire before she retired from politics in 1974.

An Israeli F4E fighter aircraft

Indira Gandhi

Indira Gandhi (1917-84) was the daughter of India's first prime minister, Nehru. At the age of 21, she became a member of the Congress party, and took a series of increasingly important jobs. In 1966, Prime Minister Lal Shastri died and Mrs. Gandhi, as she is now known, took his place.

Although she was an able politician, Mrs. Gandhi failed to deal with some of the enormous problems facing India at that time. Religious differences between groups of Muslims, Hindus and Sikhs led to fighting.

Indira Gandhi

The country suffered severe economic troubles, which were increased by a war with Pakistan. When rioting broke out, Mrs. Gandhi acted ruthlessly to regain control. She imprisoned thousands of her opponents, censored the press, and began to rule India as a dictator.

These failures, along with accusations that she had cheated, caused Mrs. Gandhi to lose an important election in 1977. But she was determined to regain political power, and embarked on a campaign that covered 63,000 km (40,000 miles) in 63 days. She spoke publicly to over 240 million Indians.

She was re-elected Prime Minister in 1980, but she remained unpopular with many people. In 1984, Mrs. Gandhi was assassinated. The killers were her own Sikh bodyguards.

Evita

The popularity of Eva Perón (1919-52) played an enormous part in the political success of her husband, Juan, who become the president of Argentina in 1946.

Before she married, Eva was a well-known singer and actress in Argentina.

A poster for a show starring Eva Perón, before she gave up her acting career.

She was a brilliant speaker, and won the trust of the people, who affectionately called her "Evita". She founded hospitals, schools, parks and swimming pools, and attempted to improve conditions for workers.

When she died from cancer aged only 33, thousands of mourners filed past her coffin.

After his wife's death, Juan Perón's popularity fell sharply, and three years later he was ousted from power. He eventually remarried and was re-elected in Argentina many years later.

Eva Perón making one of her many charismatic public speeches

The Iron Lady

Margaret Thatcher was born in England in 1925. She abandoned an early career as a research chemist to become a politician. She joined the Conservative party, and became a member of the British Parliament in 1959.

The Conservative party symbol

In 1975, she became leader of the Conservative party, and in 1979 was elected Britain's first woman prime minister. She also became the first prime minister in the 20th century to win three consecutive elections. Margaret Thatcher was renowned for her tough style of leadership, which earned her the title "the Iron Lady".

This is a view of the interior of the House of Commons, where the British Parliament meets.

The two leading parties sit on opposite sides of the House.

The nickname reflected the way she dominated other members of her government, as well as her hard line on foreign policy.

In 1982, Britain's success against Argentina in the Falklands War increased Margaret Thatcher's popularity. But she was also seen as a heartless leader who didn't care about the poor, and was criticized for not supporting other women in her government.

In 1990, many Conservatives began to fear that she wouldn't win a fourth election. She had introduced the "Poll Tax", a method of taxing people, which had made her very unpopular. Eventually members of her own party forced her to resign as prime minister.

The leaders of the parties sit on the "front benches".

Front benches

Margaret Thatcher

Cory Aquino

In 1983, Senator Benigno Aquino was shot dead in Manila in the Philippines, the victim of a political conspiracy. The Philippines were ruled by President Marcos, a corrupt dictator who used the strength of the state army to maintain power.

Marcos's wife, Imelda, owned thousands of pairs of shoes. They became a symbol of the President's corruption.

Cory Aquino, campaigning for election in the Philippines

Many Filipina people turned to Aquino's wife, Corazon Aquino (b.1933), known as Cory. They begged her to stand against Marcos in the 1986 election. The election was almost sabotaged by Marcos's supporters, but Cory was declared the winner. Some soldiers rebelled against Marcos, forcing him and his wife Imelda to flee the country, and Cory became president.

She faced enormous problems. The luxurious lifestyle enjoyed by the Marcos family had plunged the country into debt. The political system was corrupt, and many of the people suffered terrible poverty.

Cory attempted to bring a new honesty and morality to Filipina politics. She survived several attempted uprisings, but didn't stand for re-election in 1992.

FEMALE FIGHTERS

In many of the wars which have dominated history, women have taken up arms to defend their homelands and beliefs. Often they have had to disguise themselves as men to go to war.

Warrior queen

Boudicca, queen of a 1st-century British tribe called the Iceni, was one of the few leaders to defeat the mighty Roman army. When Roman troops raided Iceni territory in 60AD, they flogged Boudicca and abused her daughters. Enraged by this mistreatment, Queen Boudicca rallied her tribe for a ferocious military campaign.

Boudicca and her Iceni warriors attacked the Roman colonies of Camulodunum, Verulamium and Londinium (now the cities of Colchester, St. Albans and London). They killed 70,000 Romans.

The Roman governor of Britain gathered together an army of highly trained men. They overwhelmed the Iceni in a bloody battle. Facing defeat, Boudicca is said to have taken poison in order to avoid being captured.

One legend claims Boudicca's body is buried under platform eight of King's Cross, a railway station in London.

Far-eastern fighter

Hua Mu-lan (c.400) was the daughter of a 5th-century Chinese general. She became a fighter to protect her father. When he was called to war in his old age, Mu-lan feared for his safety. She insisted that she should go in his place, challenging him to a sword-fight, on the condition that he would allow her to go if she won.

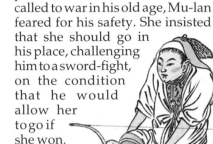

Mu-lan won the duel, proving her sword skills. Then she disguised herself as a man, and went on to spend the next 12 years fighting battles for her country.

A Chinese painting of Hua Mu-lan

Legend says that Mu-lan's courage was so admired, and her male disguise so convincing, that one Commander-in-Chief offered her his daughter in marriage.

After her career as a soldier, Mu-lan returned home and gave up fighting. She lived the rest of her life at home, as a woman.

Iceni warriors leaving the settlement of Verulamium, having defeated the Roman army

The wooden Roman settlements were easily set alight.

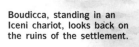

Boudicca, standing in an Iceni chariot, looks back on the ruins of the settlement.

Iceni warriors had padded tunics and oval shields.

Roman soldiers wore helmets and metal and leather tunics.

God's soldier

In the early 15th century, a peasant girl from the French village of Domrémy began to hear voices. Jeanne d'Arc (c.1412-31) believed that the voices belonged to three Christian saints. They told her to overthrow the English army that had captured the Paris region of France. She was to ensure that Charles the Dauphin, the heir to the throne, was crowned as king of France.

Jeanne's religious conviction and great confidence inspired other French people to fight the English. She gathered an army and led them to victory in a battle for the city of Orléans.

The city of Orléans was protected by high stone walls.

Jeanne leads the Dauphin's army to defeat the city of Orléans.

Jeanne dressed for battle in men's clothing.

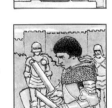
After capturing Orléans, Jeanne's army advanced to the city of Rheims, where the Dauphin was crowned.

Jeanne's sword broke while she was fighting the English near Paris. Her followers saw this as a sign of bad luck.

The English captured Jeanne and accused her of using witchcraft. She was burned at the stake in 1431.

After her death, Jeanne became a national heroine. She was eventually made a saint in 1920.

African Queen

Jinga Mbandi (c.1580-1663) was the sister of the ruler of the West African kingdom of Ndongo. She attempted to negotiate her country's independence from the Portuguese settlers who were trading in slaves there. During the negotiations with the Portuguese governor, Jinga sat on one of her servants because she wasn't offered a chair.

When her brother died, Jinga became queen. Soon after, the Portuguese drove her out of Ndongo. Jinga trained soldiers herself and fought back repeatedly.

Jinga Mbandi sitting on a servant

Soldiering on

In the 17th century, men were often seized and forceably recruited into the English army. Richard Welsh was a typical victim. His wife was less typical. Christian Welsh (1667-1739), best known as Kit Cavanagh, set out to find her husband.

Richard was made helplessly drunk, kidnapped and sent to fight French forces in the Netherlands.

Determined to rejoin her husband, Christian cut her hair, wore men's clothes and joined the army.

She spent 13 years as a soldier before finding her husband, and fought bravely in several major European battles.

Christian's true identity was only discovered by surgeons operating on a head wound she had received in combat. Even after this, she decided to stay in the army and worked as a cook. She died in a hospital for old soldiers in 1739.

REFORMERS

Many women have taken action against the injustices they have witnessed around them. They have fought, sometimes quite literally, for safety and equality for all.

New look Newgate

In 1813, having heard many stories of the appalling conditions in English prisons, Elizabeth Fry (1780-1845) visited Newgate, the largest and most notorious of London's jails. She was horrified by what she found.

Over 300 women were locked up, along with their children, in one cramped cell. Those convicted of serious crimes were held with others who were awaiting trial for minor crimes. The women were clothed in filthy rags, and had no proper beds, toilets, or washing facilities. Many of them drank heavily to try to forget the squalor.

Elizabeth began to pay regular visits to the women of Newgate. She won their trust by bringing them fresh clothes and talking kindly to them. She persuaded them to work together toward an improved standard of living.

In an empty cell, Elizabeth set up a school for the prisoners' children. She chose well-behaved inmates to keep order. She made a deal with the women that if they stopped gambling and drinking, she would find them paid work.

Elizabeth's ideas improved living conditions and prisoner discipline in Newgate to such an extent, that it was not long before other prison authorities copied her approach. She toured Europe giving lectures to promote her ideas about prison reform.

Elizabeth Fry

Soujourner Truth

Many women were involved in the struggle to abolish slavery in the USA. Isabella Van Wagener (1797-1883), an African-American woman, was born into slavery but gained her freedom in 1828, with the abolition of slavery in her home state of New York.

Isabella believed that God wanted her to fight for the abolition of slavery throughout the USA. She took the name "Sojourner Truth", which means "one who works for truth", and toured the country. Her powerful speeches drew large crowds, and helped bring about the end of American slavery.

Sojourner Truth

Before Elizabeth Fry's reforms, conditions in the cells were cramped and filthy.

Newgate Prison, with the women's wing on the right-hand side.

The women were able to earn a little money by sewing.

Elizabeth read aloud to the women to entertain and educate them.

Temperance tantrums

People who campaign against the abuse of alcohol are known as temperance workers. The most formidable was an American named Carry Nation (1846-1911). She was briefly married to an alcoholic doctor and this inspired her lifelong opposition to drink.

Carry led other temperance workers in "saloon-smashing" expeditions, when they wrecked the interiors of drinking establishments with hatchets. Despite being repeatedly imprisoned for breach of the peace, she continued to use "hatchetation" to oppose the sale of alcohol.

Carry funded her campaign and paid her many fines, by lecturing, appearing on stage, and selling souvenir hatchets.

In 1920, nine years after Carry's death a ban on alcohol, known as Prohibition, was imposed throughout the USA. However, the ban proved too hard to enforce, and was lifted in 1933.

This cartoon shows Carry Nation wielding a hatchet. Besides alcohol, she opposed corsets, short skirts, tobacco and foreign food.

Working for peace

During her lifetime, Jane Addams (1860-1935) was called both "the greatest American who ever lived" and "the most dangerous woman in the country". She devoted her life to campaigning for justice and peace for all.

In her youth, Jane trained as a doctor. When poor health forced her to give up medical school, she remained determined to help people. She witnessed the terrible conditions suffered by families

The American reformer Jane Addams (right) during her unpopular campaign for peace

who lived in the slums of Chicago. She opened Hull House, a settlement that offered help to poor immigrants. The idea caught on quickly, and local clubs were set up offering medical care, child care, and classes in English and fine arts. By 1893, there were forty clubs helping over 2000 women and girls a week.

Jane Addams lost her popularity, however, after campaigning for peace during World War I. She believed that fighting was wrong, an attitude many Americans considered very unpatriotic.

Despite violent opposition, Jane stuck to her beliefs. She set up a Woman's Peace Party in the USA and was the first President of the Women's International League for Peace and Freedom. After the fighting was over, she helped send food to Europeans who had been left poor, hungry and devastated by the war.

The Montessori Method

Maria Montessori (1870-1952) changed the way that young children all over the world were educated. After becoming the first woman in Italy to qualify as a doctor, Maria began working in a clinic in Rome with mentally handicapped children. She

Maria Montessori

realized that the oppressive style of education typical in her day wasn't very effective. She believed that using bright, attractive teaching materials, and "fun" exercises would greatly improve the children's progress.

The Italian government asked Maria to set up a *Casa dei Bambini*, or "Children's House", in a poor area of Rome. She produced impressive results by using equipment and techniques which encouraged her pupils' natural tendency to learn by play. Her success led to the adoption of the "Montessori Method" of education in children's schools around the world.

Children learning through play and fun exercises, according to the Montessori Method.

11

REVOLUTIONARIES

There have been women who lacked political power, yet inspired revolutionary movements. Their words and ideas challenged the injustice and inequality they found in the governments of their day.

Revolution and Roland

The French Revolution of 1789 was an uprising against the privileges enjoyed by the aristocrats who dominated the country. Several people were responsible for developing the ideas of equality and liberty that led to the revolution. One was a woman named Manon Roland (1754-93).

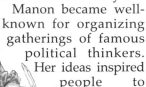

Manon believed that French citizens of all classes should be treated equally. She hoped that revolution would end the unfairness in society.

Manon became well-known for organizing gatherings of famous political thinkers. Her ideas inspired people to overthrow the ruling classes. When revolution came, King Louis XVI and many aristocrats were executed by guillotine. A group of extreme anti-royalists called the Jacobins seized power. They hated Manon because she had been against the King's execution. Despite supporting the revolution, Manon was sent to the guillotine.

Manon Roland

Crowds gather to watch an execution.

Voice of the people

Alexandra Kollontai (1872-1952) witnessed the terrible conditions suffered by workers and decided to devote her life to bringing about a revolution in her native Russia.

In 1896, Alexandra visited a textile factory in Finland. She was shocked by the workers' terrible conditions and long hours.

Back home in Russia, she saw the Czar's troops killing hundreds of workers who were peacefully demonstrating.

Alexandra made speeches calling for fair conditions for workers and freedom for women. But the secret police were watching her.

Alexandra was continually harassed for her political activities, so she fled abroad in 1908. She didn't return until 1917, after revolution had broken out and the Czar had been deposed.

In Russia's new government, she became Commissar for Public Welfare. But her outspoken views made her unpopular and she was sent abroad to help foreign trade. Finally, in Sweden, she became the first ever female ambassador.

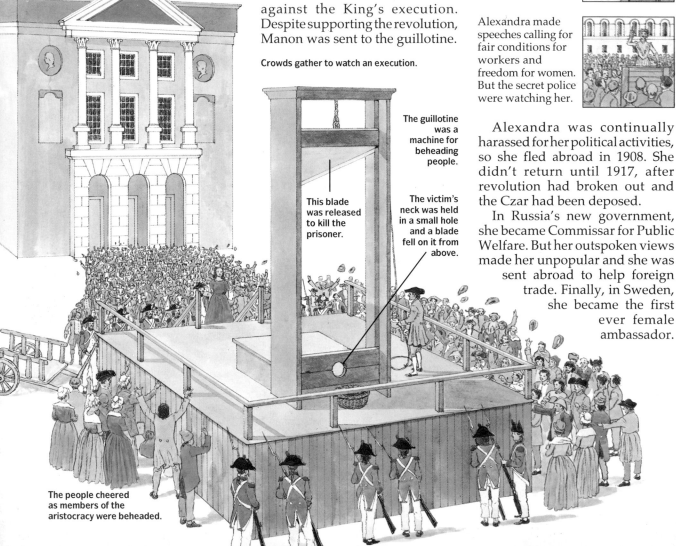

The guillotine was a machine for beheading people.

This blade was released to kill the prisoner.

The victim's neck was held in a small hole and a blade fell on it from above.

The people cheered as members of the aristocracy were beheaded.

Red Rosa

Polish-born Rosa Luxemburg (1870-1919) was a devoted believer in the ideals of communism, which aims for a society without classes and with common ownership of property. After she had moved to Germany in 1898, Rosa began to organize many revolts and strikes, urging workers to challenge their bosses.

Rosa Luxemburg

Rosa was jailed repeatedly for her beliefs. She was even given the nickname "Red Rosa", because red was associated with communism.

In 1914, she set up an anti-war organization known as the Spartacus League. The League campaigned for an end to international wars, encouraging the German people to overthrow their government instead.

In January 1919, members of the League attempted an uprising. When it failed, Rosa went into hiding. She was found by soldiers, beaten and shot. However, her political writings continued to be very influential long after her death.

During her many prison sentences, Rosa was able to develop and write about her political ideas.

Freedom fighter

At the beginning of the 20th century, Ireland was governed by the British Parliament, based in London. Many Irish people wanted their country to have its own government. They were known as Republicans. Constance Markiewiecz (1876-1927) was one of their most famous and popular leaders.

Constance Markiewiecz

In 1916, Constance took part in the Easter Rising, in which Republican and British forces clashed at St. Stephen's Green in Dublin, the Irish capital. She marched at the head of a column of 120 Irish soldiers. Together, they fought for three days before being forced to surrender.

Constance leads the Republican soldiers to St. Stephen's Green.

Constance was sent to prison in England for her part in the Easter Rising. She was so popular, however, that in 1918 the people of Dublin elected her as their Member of Parliament. This made her the first woman ever to be elected. Constance refused to take up her seat, however, because she was opposed to British rule in Ireland.

Under house arrest

In 1988, a young woman named Aung San Suu Kyi (b.1945) became aware of the injustices being committed by the military leaders of Myanmar (formerly Burma). She decided to fight for the people's right to choose their own government, forming a political party called the National League for Democracy.

Suu Kyi showed great courage in her political activities. Once, soldiers threatened to shoot her for walking down a road. When she refused to stop, they aimed their guns, but two officers stopped them from firing.

For six years, Suu Kyi was under house arrest, unable to leave her house, or see her family who lived in Britain. Sometimes she didn't even have enough to eat. In 1990, her party won an election, although the authorities ignored the result, and in 1991 she was awarded a Nobel peace prize.

Suu Kyi was released from house arrest in July 1995 and began to campaign again. Despite regaining her freedom, she remains under surveillance and as yet, the Government have refused to hold meetings with her and her supporters.

Suu Kyi speaking to her supporters in 1995

WOMEN HELPING WOMEN

Throughout history, women have lacked rights and have been treated as inferior to men. While many women have put up with this, some have protested against unfair treatment and urged others to do the same. This kind of protest became the basis for modern feminism.

Speaking out

One of the first marches for women's rights was led by a Roman woman named Hortensia. In 43BC, a civil war was raging throughout the Roman Empire. Mark Antony, the leader of one of the factions, decided to raise funds for the war by taxing 1,400 wealthy women. The women refused to pay for a war which involved Romans fighting each other.

Mark Antony's head on a coin

They wanted the chance for their political opinions to be heard by the government, so they marched to the Forum, a meeting place in Rome, to put their case. Hortensia was their spokeswoman. She succeeded in persuading the Roman governors to reduce the number of women taxed to 400.

Hortensia meets the governors of Rome at the steps of the Forum.

Suffragettes

In most countries, women were denied suffrage – the right to vote in political elections – until the 20th century. In Britain, Emmeline Pankhurst (1857-1928) and her daughter, Christabel (1880-1958), were among the first to fight for votes for women. They were known as suffragettes.

At first, Emmeline organized peaceful marches, demonstrations and appeals to Members of Parliament. When this didn't work, she and her followers turned to more extreme methods.

Some suffragettes chained themselves to the railings outside the Prime Minister's residence.

Some broke windows in Parliament and shouted at Members from boats on the River Thames.

A suffragette named Emily Davison threw herself under the King's racehorse in the 1913 Derby and was killed.

Emmeline and her fellow suffragettes were often arrested. In prison, they went on hunger strike. This seriously damaged Emmeline's health.

The symbol of the Women's Social and Political Union, founded by the Pankhursts in 1903

Emmeline Pankhurst being arrested

When World War I broke out in 1914, the suffragettes halted their campaign. Emmeline devoted her energy to recruiting soldiers. It was partly the contribution of women to the war effort that persuaded the government to grant them suffrage. In 1918, women over 30 were given the vote. In 1928, two weeks after Emmeline's death, the age was lowered to 21, finally making women equal to men.

The protestors gathered in the square.

Hortensia

Woman's army

As a child, Ch'iu Chin (1879-1907) realized that women in China were dependent on the men in their families and had very little freedom. Even the law said women were inferior to men. Blaming the Manchus, who had ruled for over 300 years, Chin decided to spend her life fighting for women's rights.

In 1904, Chin left her famly to study politics in Japan. It was an extreme step for a Chinese woman to take at this time.

By wearing men's clothes and learning to ride and use a sword, she encouraged women to behave as they pleased.

As part of her revolutionary plan to overthrow the Manchus, Chin learned how to fight and make bombs.

When she returned to China, Chin taught at a college. She set up a newspaper for women, and organized her students into a women's army. Government troops searched the college and found stashes of ammunition and weapons. Chin was arrested in 1907 and beheaded immediately.

Four years later, there was a revolution in China. The new rulers had a different attitude toward women. They praised Chin for the part she had played in preparing women for revolution.

Ch'iu Chin's photograph shown on a poster

Gaining control

While she was nursing in New York, Margaret Sanger (1883-1966) saw many of the difficulties facing women with large families. Many women endured poor conditions and ill-health. Her own mother had died at the age of 49, leaving 11 children.

Margaret encouraged women to limit the size of their families by using contraception – ways to prevent pregnancy. She came up with the name "birth control" to describe this process.

In a pamphlet called *Family Limitation*, she gave advice on how to use contraception. At that time, spreading information about birth control was illegal. When she opened a birth control clinic, Margaret was sent to prison.

She started the American Birth Control League, striving to gain political support for her views.

Margaret Sanger (left) outside the court where she was tried

Gradually, the law and public opinion began to change, and the number of birth control clinics grew. In 1937, the law finally allowed doctors to prescribe contraceptives.

Modern forms of contraception

Strong words

The French novelist and philosopher Simone de Beauvoir (1908-86) was a hugely influential feminist.

In 1949, she set out her ideas in a book called *The Second Sex*. Controversially, she argued that motherhood, marriage and social conditioning imprisoned women. The book became an international bestseller and a focus for the women's movement.

Simone believed that it was time for women to choose their own roles in society, which included deciding whether they wanted to have children. She argued that contraception should be easily available, and spoke in support of abortion. In 1974, she became president of the League for the Rights of Women and campaigned for help for battered wives, working women and single parents.

Simone de Beauvoir

With her lifelong companion, the philosopher Jean-Paul Sartre, Simone helped to set up a political newspaper, *Les Temps Modernes* ("Modern Times"). She was photographed around the world, meeting leaders who supported her political beliefs.

Although Simone's views were controversial, she was recognized in France as a heroine. In 1986, French radio interrupted broadcasts to announce her death.

ROBBERS AND ROGUES

Women are not generally known for breaking the law. Even today, male criminals vastly outnumber female ones. A few notorious women, however, are remembered for their crimes.

Moll Cutpurse

Mary Frith (c.1590-1659) was a pickpocket who chose her victims on the streets of London. In her day, people often carried their money in purses tied around their waists. Thieves would secretly cut the ties to steal the purses. Frith was so good at this that she gained the nickname "Moll Cutpurse".

Later, Moll found that she could make even more money buying stolen goods from other thieves, and then selling them for a higher price.

She sold her booty in a "second-hand" shop. The shop was visited both by robbers and by their victims, who came to buy back their stolen possessions.

Moll became so well-known that, by the time she was 26, she was made the subject of a successful play, entitled *The Roaring Girle*.

A drawing of Moll from a poster advertising The Roaring Girle

The Bandit Queen

In the 19th century, the cowboy towns of the American "Wild West" produced several women bank robbers, swindlers, and cattle thieves. The most famous of these was the outlaw known as Belle Starr (1848-89) who became the subject of many stories and legends.

Belle Starr

She eloped with another outlaw, Jim Reed. In Texas, they took part in a famous stagecoach hold-up. But Reed was killed in a gun-fight a year later.

In 1880, Belle got married again, to the outlaw Sam Starr. They settled in Oklahoma together to pursue a life of crime.

Belle lived in a cabin she called Younger's Bend. It became a popular hideout for outlaws such as Jesse James.

She led a gang of outlaws that met at Younger's Bend to plan robberies. The newspapers called Belle "The Bandit Queen".

She masterminded several raids to steal horses. But thanks to her legal skills, Belle only went to prison once for her crimes.

The U.S. government offered thousands of dollars for Belle's capture, but she still survived longer than many of her fellow outlaws. In 1889, she was captured and stories circulated that her own son shot her dead in an ambush at Younger's Bend.

A poster issued by the United States government for the capture of Belle Starr

Mata Hari

Margarete Zelle (1876-1917) moved from the Netherlands to live in Java, in the East Indies, when she was 19 years old. There she learned the skills of exotic eastern-style dancing. With her new talent, she decided to go to France to become a dancer.

She gave herself the stage name "MataHari", which means "child of the dawn" in Javanese. She became well-known for her sensational performances in Paris.

Many important men sent her gifts, and before long she was a very wealthy woman. In 1914, however, World War I broke out and Mata Hari embarked on a new profession as a spy.

Mata Hari in an exotic dancing costume

In 1917, the French government accused her of coaxing military secrets from her lovers and sending the information to their German enemies. Mata Hari insisted that she had been spying for the French, but nobody believed her. She was executed by a firing squad. Some people still believe that she was innocent.

Mata Hari awaits execution by a firing squad in 1917.

Bonnie and Clyde

The American waitress Bonnie Parker (1911-34) and her lover Clyde Barrow were infamous criminals. At first they only committed petty crimes, such as burglary and theft, but they went on to bank robbery and murder.

At one point Barrow was sent to prison for two years. Bonnie managed to get a pistol smuggled into jail for him. He used it to escape.

Barrow was recaptured and was transferred to a much tougher jail, known by its prisoners as "Burning Hell".

As soon as Barrow was released, he and Bonnie started to gather other criminals together to form the "Barrow Gang".

Working with the Barrow Gang, they stole guns from a government weaponry, and used them in a series of robberies and killings.

Bonnie and Clyde fooling around with a machine gun

Bonnie and Clyde became famous throughout America. In 1934, they died in a hail of bullets as they drove into a police ambush.

Bonnie and Clyde were ambushed by police while driving a gang car.

The Beautiful Robber

Phoolan Devi (b.1963) is known throughout northern India as "The Beautiful Robber". When she was only 16, Phoolan ran away from her bullying husband and joined a gang of bandits. The gang's leader, Vikram Mallah, taught Phoolan how to use weapons and camouflage.

In 1980, two members of the gang, the Singh brothers, shot Mallah dead and took Phoolan prisoner. They beat and abused her for three weeks, until she managed to escape.

Phoolan soon took over the leadership of another gang of bandits. She led her gang in a revenge attack against the Singhs' home village, killing 24 of the Singhs' relatives and friends.

Thousands of policemen pursued Phoolan for over two years, before she finally gave herself up.

Phoolan held by police after giving herself up

Since her arrest, Phoolan Devi has become better known for her political opinions than for her crimes. When she was released in 1994, she began a political campaign to seek election.

Bullet holes in the side of the car after the ambush.

BRAVE AND BOLD WOMEN

Many women have shown remarkable courage in the face of adversity, often putting their own lives at risk to save others. Their heroic deeds have ensured their lasting fame.

Black Moses

In the mid-19th century, slavery was outlawed in the northern American states, but in the South it was still permitted. Black slaves in the South tried to escape to freedom in the North by following a route known as the "Underground Railroad".

There were some people along this route who disagreed with slavery. They provided the escaping slaves with food, clothing and shelter.

Slaves wore tags like this to show who they were.

The Railroad had "conductors", who guided escapees on their journey to the northern states and Canada where they would be safe from recapture. The most famous conductor was a woman named Harriet Tubman (c.1820-1913).

Harriet had escaped from slavery herself and she repeatedly risked recapture by leading slaves to freedom. Among the 300 people she helped were several members of her family. Angry slave-owners offered huge rewards for her capture.

Harriet was given the nickname "Black Moses", after Moses in the Bible, who led his people, the Israelites, to the safety of the Promised Land.

In this poster of 1853, a trader offers $1,200 or more for black slaves, who were at that time known as "negroes".

The rebellious Rani

British forces spent much of the 19th century trying to force the people of India to accept British rule. In an uprising known as the Indian Mutiny, several Indian states raised armies against the British. A woman named Lakshmi Bai (1835-57) became famous for her heroism during the Mutiny.

Lakshmi was married to the ruler, or *Raja*, of the Indian state of Jhansi, and took the title of *Rani*.

When the Raja died, Britain declared that Jhansi couldn't remain an independent state, but had to accept British rule.

This picture of Lakshmi Bai, the Rani of Jhansi, was painted in 1890.

Lakshmi protested to the British, but to no avail. So, at the outbreak of the Mutiny, she led Indian troops into battle. She fought courageously, wearing a soldier's uniform, wielding a two-handed sword, and holding the reins of her horse in her teeth, but was cut down by a British cavalryman.

Talking fingers

A less dramatic, but no less heroic, story is that of an American woman named Helen Keller (1880-1968), who showed great courage in overcoming severe disabilities. As a baby, she suffered from a disease called scarlet fever which left her totally blind and profoundly deaf. Helen's parents found an extraordinary teacher named Anne Sullivan to help Helen.

Harriet Tubman, who was nicknamed "Black Moses" for helping slaves escape.

This map of the United States of America shows the states in which slavery was still permitted in 1844.

■ States where slavery was permitted

Helen Keller "listened" to the radio by touching its case with her fingers to feel the vibrations.

Anne, who was partially sighted herself, proved to be a wonderful teacher. Under her guidance, Helen learned to read Braille and communicate using special finger movements to spell words into another person's palm. She could understand speech by placing her fingertips on a speaker's lips while they spoke.

Helen attended college and gained a degree with distinction. She was accompanied at all times by her teacher. In later life, she gave lectures on how disabilities such as hers could be overcome. Her relentless campaigning in aid of the American Foundation for the Blind raised over two million dollars. Her work promoted public awareness of the challenges faced by blind and deaf people all around the world.

This Braille watch has raised bumps which enable blind people to tell the time.

Against all odds

In the 1930s, an English woman named Gladys Aylward (1902-70) was working as a missionary in northern China. When Japanese soldiers invaded the region, Aylward went to work as a governess at a home for war orphans. She devoted herself to helping the Chinese army by spying for them. When the Japanese realized what she was doing, they came after her.

As Gladys fled from the Japanese soldiers across a graveyard, one of them shot her in the back. Fortunately, she was protected by her traditional, thickly padded Chinese coat.

Gladys Aylward's passport

Although the bullet knocked her over, it didn't seriously injure her. Quickly, she wriggled out of her coat and hid in a ditch. The soldiers shot at the coat again, thinking Gladys was still wearing it. Finally they went, presuming that she was dead.

Gladys decided that she must evacuate the war orphans in her school, and take them to the safety of Sian, in western China. She and over a hundred children set off on a two-month trek that took them over the mountains and across the Yellow River. They were helped by a group of Chinese soldiers, who gave them much-needed food and transportation. On one stretch of the journey, the children had to hide in coal wagons to avoid the Japanese troops. Against all odds, Gladys and her group finally reached Sian unharmed.

Gladys Aylward led her band of children to safety across many miles of Chinese countryside.

Secret agent

During World War II, some French citizens secretly gathered to oppose the German invaders. They formed the Resistance Movement. Violette Szabo was one of many British agents sent to help them. She was dropped into France by parachute in June 1944.

Violette parachuting into enemy territory

Violette sacrificed her life when she and a Resistance leader named Anastasie were ambushed by Germans.

As the two women fled through a cornfield, Violette stumbled and sprained her ankle. She couldn't go any farther.

Insisting that Anastasie went on, Violette crawled to the edge of the field, stood up, and opened fire on the soldiers.

She held their attention until Anastasie could escape. Finally, she ran out of ammunition and was captured.

Just two months before the war ended, Violette Szabo was shot. After her death, she was awarded medals for the incredible bravery she had shown.

NOTORIOUS WOMEN

The despicable deeds of certain women have ensured their lasting infamy. Some women are deservedly notorious for their crimes; in other cases their evil deeds have been exaggerated.

Popes and poison

Lucrezia Borgia (1480-1519) belonged to an Italian family that was renowned for merciless political scheming. Her father's ruthless plotting led him to become Pope Alexander VI.

By the time she was in her early 20s, Lucrezia had been married three times. Many people believed that she was also involved in a number of scandalous love affairs.

She was even said to be a witch, who had killed many people using special rings containing poisoned capsules. According to the stories, she slipped these capsules secretly into her victims' drinks.

Rings containing capsules of poison

After her marriage to the Duke of Ferrara, Lucrezia established her court as a place where many poets, writers, musicians and painters would gather.

Lucrezia Borgia probably didn't deserve her bad reputation. It is likely that she was accused of these crimes because of the unpopularity of several other members of her family. Despite this, however, she continued to have a reputation as a villainess.

Lucrezia Borgia was used as a model for the figure of Saint Catherine in this painting.

Bloody Mary

Mary Tudor (1516-1558), the daughter of Henry VIII and Katherine of Aragon, became Queen Mary I of England in 1553.

At this time, the country was divided between Catholics and Protestants members of the Anglican Church, set up by Henry VIII as the official Church of England.

Mary was a very devout Catholic, and several Protestant noblemen wanted to keep her out of power. Before Mary could take the throne, they crowned a 16-year-old named Lady Jane Grey, the great-granddaughter of Henry VII. After only nine days, Mary Tudor sent her troops to arrest Jane, and took the throne for herself.

Jane and her husband were beheaded on Tower Green in the Tower of London.

Queen Mary I of England

This marked the beginning of Mary's reign of terror. She planned to crush any rebellions, wipe out Protestantism, and restore Catholicism as the state religion in England. On her instructions, many Protestants were put on trial, including Thomas Cranmer, the Archbishop of Canterbury. They were accused of being heretics, because they refused to practise Catholicism. Those who were found guilty were burned at the stake.

Over 300 people were put to death during the five years of Mary's reign. For her cruelty and willingness to execute people, she was given the title "Bloody Mary".

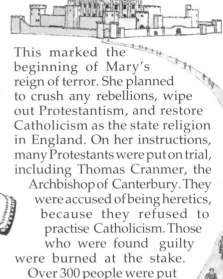

The Tower of London, site of many executions

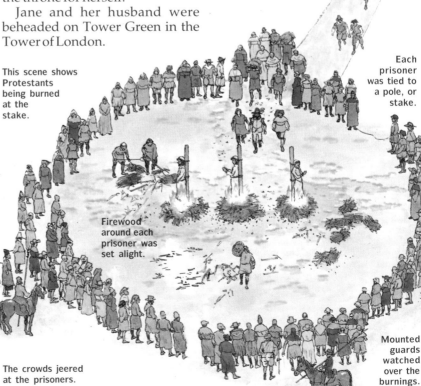

This scene shows Protestants being burned at the stake.

Firewood around each prisoner was set alight.

The crowds jeered at the prisoners.

Each prisoner was tied to a pole, or stake.

Mounted guards watched over the burnings.

Rat poison

At the age of 22, a Scottish woman named Madeleine Smith (1835-1928) agreed to marry William Kinnoch, a wealthy local businessman. But Madeleine was already secretly engaged to another man.

Madeleine's fiancé was a warehouse clerk named Pierre Emile L'Angelier. L'Angelier tried desperately to prevent her from marrying Kinnoch. He even threatened to show her father the passionate love letters that he had received from her.

Madeleine Smith

One of the letters sent by Madeleine to L'Angelier, which he used to blackmail her.

Pierre Emile L'Angelier

On several occasions, L'Angelier demanded that Madeleine meet him, and tried to persuade her to marry him instead of Kinnoch. After one of these meetings, in March 1857, L'Angelier died suddenly and painfully. When tests on his body showed that he had been poisoned by repeated doses of a deadly chemical called arsenic, Madeleine became the prime murder suspect.

She had an obvious motive for wanting to kill L'Angelier quickly, so that she could marry her wealthier suitor. The police also discovered that she had bought arsenic from a local chemist's shop three times shortly before the murder. But Madeleine claimed that she had used the arsenic to poison some rats that were infesting her house.

She was brilliantly defended by a top lawyer in what became one of the 19th century's most sensational trials. She eventually walked free after the jury returned a verdict of "not proven".

Nursery crimes

In 1892, Lizzie Borden (1860-1927) was accused of a double murder. The victims were her father and stepmother, killed with an axe at their home in Fall River, Massachusetts. The only other people in the house at the time were Lizzie and an Irish maid.

Almost a year after the murders, Lizzie Borden was put on trial. There was a lot of very strong evidence against her.

She had often argued with her father over his meanness, and had argued bitterly with her stepmother.

The axe was found in the Bordens' cellar, and Lizzie had been seen burning a dress, which may have been bloodstained.

Nevertheless, Lizzie was found not guilty because there was not enough evidence to convict her. Despite the hostility of the townspeople, she lived in Fall River for the rest of her life.

Today, children in America still sing a nursery rhyme that tells the story of Lizzie Borden's terrible crime. The words of the rhyme are shown below.

Lizzie Borden took an axe, Gave her mother forty whacks; When she saw what she had done She gave her father forty-one.

Terror tactics

In May 1970, Ulrike Meinhof (1934-76) helped Andreas Baader, a West German terrorist, to escape from prison. Baader had been arrested for setting fire to department stores in protest against German industrialists, government policies and American forces in Germany. When Ulrike, who was a journalist, interviewed Baader in prison, he convinced her that violent action was necessary to bring about political change.

She became a leader of a group called the *Röte Armee Fraktion* (Red Army Faction), which became known as the Baader-Meinhof gang. They robbed banks, planted bombs, and carried out political assassinations in an attempt to damage the government.

The Red Army Faction symbol

Ulrike Meinhof was finally arrested in June 1972 and sentenced to eight years in prison. On 9 May 1976, however, she committed suicide in her cell at Stammheim high-security prison.

Ulrike's arrest

CAREGIVERS

Looking after the sick has traditionally been seen as a woman's job, and millions of unknown women have spent their lives as carers. Few, however, have gained fame for their dedication and determination.

Medicine man

One of the most unusual medical careers was that of Dr. James Barry (c.1795-1865). Dr. Barry was an English woman named Miranda Stewart.

In the early 19th century, women weren't allowed to study medicine. But by dressing as a man

Miranda Stewart

and using a false name, Miranda gained a place at medical school. In 1812, she became a fully qualified doctor, and by 1858, she was Inspector General of Hospitals.

Miranda had a long career. Her true identity was only discovered in 1865, when her body was examined after her death.

A selection of surgical tools

The Lady of the Lamp

In 1854, Turkish, French and British soldiers joined forces to fight the Russian army. The war was fought in an area near the Black Sea known as the Crimea. As the number of wounded men increased, nurses were desperately needed.

Florence Nightingale (1820-1910) came from a wealthy English family. She was much admired in London for her nursing work. Sidney Herbert, the Secretary of State for War, asked Florence to gather a team of nurses and set sail for the Crimea.

When she arrived in Turkey, Florence was appalled by the conditions in Scutari Barrack Hospital. She worked 20-hour shifts, converting the filthy, rat-infested wards into a cleaner, brighter, more efficient hospital.

Inside the Barrack Hospital in Scutari

A map of the Crimea and the Black Sea, showing Scutari

Florence's work at the hospital reduced the patient death rate from 42 per cent to just over 2 per cent.

Her patients adored her. They called her "the lady of the lamp" because of her habit of roaming the wards at night with a lantern, checking on their comfort and welfare.

By the time Florence returned to England, she was a national heroine.

She went on to write about the importance of diet and sanitation for good health. She also began raising money, which she used to found a nursing college, the Nightingale Training School for Nurses, in London.

Florence Nightingale's lamp

In 1907, Florence Nightingale became the first woman to be awarded the Order of Merit, which is given to British citizens in recognition of a great contribution to society.

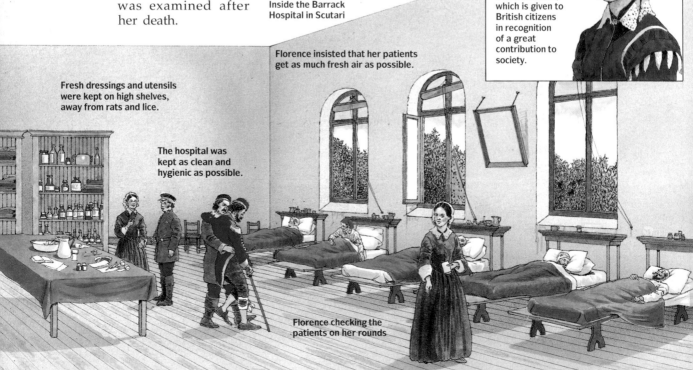

Fresh dressings and utensils were kept on high shelves, away from rats and lice.

The hospital was kept as clean and hygienic as possible.

Florence insisted that her patients get as much fresh air as possible.

Florence checking the patients on her rounds

A dedicated nurse

A Jamaican woman named Mary Seacole (1805-81) became a nurse in 1850, during an outbreak of a disease called cholera. A few years later, she sailed to England to offer her services as a Crimean War nurse, but was turned down because she was black.

Mary Seacole, depicted in an 1857 issue of *Punch*, a popular English magazine

Undeterred, Mary paid for her own passage to the Crimea, and spent the next three years working with Florence Nightingale, providing medical care for the war casualties.

When she returned to England, Mary was praised for her bravery by the same people who had previously rejected her help.

Soldiering on

When German forces invaded Belgium at the outbreak of World War I, a British nurse named Edith Cavell (1865-1915) was teaching at a nursing school in Brussels.

The school Edith worked at was turned into a Red Cross hospital for wounded soldiers.

This image is from a French memorial to Edith Cavell.

Despite the constant threat of being discovered by the German army, Edith and her staff assisted wounded British, French and Belgian soldiers. She helped them to reach Holland, where they could rejoin the Allied Army.

Under cover of darkness, the soldiers would be secretly smuggled into the Red Cross hospital.

Edith carefully disguised them as hospital patients and treated those who were wounded.

By supplying them with false identification papers and civilian clothes, she helped over 200 soldiers to safety.

For her part in helping Allied soldiers to escape the Nazis, Edith Cavell was arrested, put on trial and sentenced to death. She was shot at dawn by a German firing squad in 1915.

Mother Theresa

One woman who has become internationally famous for caring for others is Agnes Bojaxhiu (b.1910), now known as Mother Theresa. At the age of 18, she left Yugoslavia and went to work in a convent in Calcutta, India. She took a new religious name, Sister Theresa.

Over the next 20 years, Sister Theresa worked as a teacher at the convent's school and at a school for poor children.

On September 10, 1946, a day known by her followers as "Inspiration Day", Sister Theresa heard a voice from God. It told her to help Calcutta's poor by living among them. So she moved into one of the city's worst slum areas and began teaching and nursing the poor and the sick. Her pupils and patients called her "Ma", or "Mother".

Mother Theresa was joined by other women who wanted to help the poor. As their numbers grew, they became known as the "Sisters of Charity". They set up their own hospital, Nirmal Hriday, which means "The Place of the Pure Heart".

In 1979, Mother Theresa was awarded the Nobel peace prize for the work she had done to set up Missionaries of Charity, a worldwide religious organization which cares for people anywhere in the world who are destitute or dying.

A Nobel peace prize medal

Mother Theresa works and cares for the people of Calcutta, many of whom live in great poverty.

THE POWER BEHIND THE THRONE

Behind many of history's powerful men there have been powerful women. Among these are some women whose popularity or political skills have made them as famous, if not more famous, than their husbands.

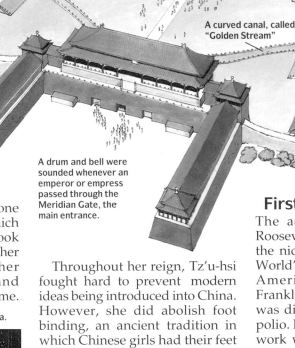

The city is guarded by bronze lions like this one.

Tz'u-hsi sat on the Dragon throne in the Hall of Supreme Harmony.

A curved canal, called "Golden Stream"

The Hall of Supreme Harmony is raised on a three-tiered terrace.

The central area of the Forbidden City in Beijing, the largest palace in the world. It has 8,000 rooms.

A drum and bell were sounded whenever an emperor or empress passed through the Meridian Gate, the main entrance.

The Old Buddha

At the age of 16, Tz'u-hsi (1835-1908) was taken into the Forbidden City in Beijing, to become one of the wives of Emperor Hsien-feng. She soon became the Emperor's close friend, and even advised him on State affairs.

When the Emperor died in 1861, Tz'u-hsi claimed the throne for her son. Despite a law which forbade women to reign, she took political control herself. When her son died, she appointed her nephew as Emperor and continued to govern in his name.

Tz'u-hsi was also known as the Old Buddha.

Throughout her reign, Tz'u-hsi fought hard to prevent modern ideas being introduced into China. However, she did abolish foot binding, an ancient tradition in which Chinese girls had their feet tightly bound to keep them small, which was considered attractive. Many women were crippled by this practice.

This woman's feet have been crippled by years of tight binding.

Tz'u-hsi ruled for over 50 years. She was a formidable figure to the last, and even organized the murder of her nephew, the Emperor, a day before she died.

First Lady of the World

The achievements of Eleanor Roosevelt (1884-1962) earned her the nickname "First Lady of the World". She was the wife of an American politician named Franklin D. Roosevelt. In 1921, he was disabled by a disease called polio. Eleanor took on his political work while he was ill. With her support, Roosevelt went on to become President of the United States in 1932.

President Roosevelt died in 1945. In the same year, a special council called the United Nations, or UN, was set up to promote international peace and co-operation. Eleanor Roosevelt was elected to be its American representative.

The UN symbol

Eleanor Roosevelt holding up a copy of the Declaration of Human Rights

In 1948, Eleanor led a committee which persuaded 48 countries to sign the Universal Declaration of Human Rights. This outlined the rights of all people to liberty and justice. For her commitment to human rights, the American public repeatedly voted her "Most Admired Woman of the Year".

Jackie Kennedy

The popularity and charm of Jackie Kennedy (1929-1994) contributed enormously to the success of her husband, John F. Kennedy, (Jack). He was President of the United States from 1960 until his assassination in Texas in 1963.

On November 22, the Kennedys were in Dallas, Texas, waving to the crowds from an open-top car, when Jack was shot.

Jackie panicked, and immediately tried to scramble out of the car to escape the assassin's bullets.

She insisted on wearing her bloodstained clothes at the ceremony to swear in a new president.

Jackie earned America's respect for her dignity as a widow. But she was criticized when she married a wealthy Greek ship owner named Aristotle Onassis. Some people thought she was being greedy and betraying her first husband's memory.

In her final years, Jackie worked for a publishing company in New York. She died of cancer in 1994 and was buried as a national heroine.

She who strives

Winnie Mandela (b.1934) worked hard to help her husband Nelson become president of South Africa in 1994. In 1964, Nelson had been sentenced to life imprisonment for leading a campaign of defiance against the South African government and its racist policies. Winnie campaigned tirelessly to keep her husband's name in the public eye during his long imprisonment.

Racial segregation, as shown by this sign, was supported by law in South Africa.

Winnie's African name is Nomzamo, which means "she who strives". This proved a fitting name, as she was often imprisoned, threatened and had her freedom restricted during her campaign.

Nelson was released in 1990. Later, he and Winnie divorced, because he didn't want to be associated with Winnie's controversial methods of political activity.

The Mandelas celebrating Nelson's release in 1990

Princess Diana

Diana, Princess of Wales, is one famous wife who has completely overshadowed her husband in terms of popularity and star quality. In 1981, she married Charles, Prince of Wales, the heir to the British throne, and became one of the world's most recognized faces.

A sapphire pendant and ring belonging to the Princess of Wales

She became a showpiece for British fashion. Crowds were often more eager to meet Diana than other members of the royal family. Wherever she went, she was photographed by the press.

Her popularity increased as she gave her support to charities which aimed to combat Aids, drug abuse and poverty.

However, her marriage was an unhappy one. In 1995, Diana gave a famous television interview in which she revealed many very personal details about her life. She has been accused of using her great popularity to manipulate the press. In 1996, the couple divorced.

Diana is famous for her fashionable style.

ADVENTURES OVERSEAS

Until the 19th century, it was very unusual for women to travel anywhere alone. A few women, however, set off on great explorations and became famous through written accounts of their adventures.

Hatshepsut

Egyptian Queen Hatshepsut was not an explorer herself, but sponsored a great expedition. In 1493 BC, she ordered a fleet of vessels to set sail for Punt, a land on the east coast of Africa (roughly where Somalia is today). The route had not been explored for over 200 years. The expedition's goal was to find myrrh trees, from which the Egyptians made incense to burn at religious ceremonies.

The adventures of the seamen were recorded on the walls of Hatshepsut's temple, Deir el-Bahari. Here they are shown with myrrh trees.

Even though the Egyptians had never attempted an expedition of this scale before, it was a great success and the ships came home laden with myrrh and ivory.

Travel addict

After the death of her parents, an English woman named Mary Kingsley (1862-1900) set sail for West Africa. She intended to continue her father's scientific work there, but she quickly became addicted to travel.

Even in Africa, Mary wore a heavy skirt, a high-necked blouse, and took an umbrella.

In 1893, Mary sailed along the coast of West Africa in a cargo boat. She was fascinated by the many ports she visited. On her journeys, which took her along rivers and through swamps and thick jungles, she collected specimens of fish and beetles for the British Museum in London.

Specimens of beetles and freshwater fish taken from drawings made by Mary Kingsley

Mary explored alone, except for her native guides. She ate snakes and saw wild animals such as gorillas and elephants.

Once she was saved from death by her heavy skirts when she fell five metres (15 feet) onto a spike in a game pit.

In one hut belonging to a tribe of cannibals, she found a bag containing three big toes, four eyes and two ears.

When war broke out in South Africa, Mary worked in a hospital nursing soldiers. She died of a fever and was buried at sea.

Travels on a yak

The first expeditions Alexandra David-Neel (1868-1969) ever made were when she ran away from home several times as a child. On one occasion, she went from her home in France all the way to England.

In 1911, Alexandra set off on a short trip to India, but she ended up staying abroad for 14 years. Her travels took her through Burma, Japan, Korea, the Gobi Desert and Mongolia.

Alexandra was always accompanied by her adopted son, Yongden, who was a Buddhist priest. On one trip, they covered 3200km (2000 miles) to reach a monastery on the border of China and Tibet, where Alexandra studied Buddhism for three years.

In Tibet, Alexandra sometimes rode a yak.

This is a reconstruction of one of the Egyptian trading galleys that Hatshepsut sent to the land of Punt.

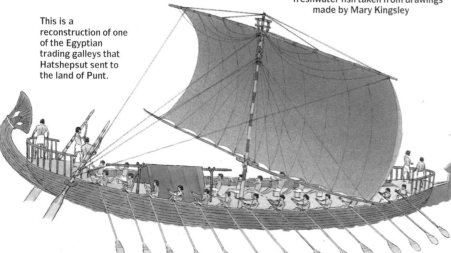

The Potala palace in Lhasa, Tibet

Alexandra's greatest journey, to Tibet, began when she was 54 years old. She crossed the country disguised as a Tibetan nun, to hide the fact that she was a foreigner. She dyed her hair black and darkened her face with cocoa. When she arrived in the capital, Lhasa, she was the first European woman ever to enter the city.

Desert adventure

As a result of her expeditions, Gertrude Bell (1868-1926), the daughter of a wealthy English family, became an expert mountaineer and a famous archeologist. In 1913, she set off for Arabia, the last great region of the world which had not been fully mapped.

Gertrude ignored warnings about dangerous desert conditions and set out for the city of Ha'il. While crossing the Syrian desert, her party was attacked by Arab horsemen. Gertrude remained calm and later described the attack as "a preposterous and provoking episode".

A map showing the route Gertrude Bell took to reach the city of Ha'il

When she reached Ha'il, Gertrude became only the second European woman to visit the mud-walled city. The ruler, Ibn Rashid, welcomed Gertrude, but then kept her in his palace, virtually as a prisoner. When she couldn't stand her confinement any longer, she announced in fluent Arabic that she was leaving. The Arab authorities were so stunned by this that they let her go.

This is a reconstruction of the attack on Gertrude Bell's group by a gang of Arab horsemen.

The men rode toward Gertrude, waving swords and rifles.

Gertrude was riding a camel, while her guides were on foot.

Ibn Rashid even gave Gertrude supplies and guides to help her on the difficult journey through the desert back to Damascus.

Gertrude Bell's account of her trip contributed enormously to Western knowledge of Arabian history, and the research she carried out on her travels helped geographers make more detailed maps of the Syrian desert.

Gertrude would have had an sextant like this to help her calculate distances.

Daring Dame

Dame Freya Stark (1893-1993) is probably the most famous female adventurer of the 20th century.

While working in Baghdad, she explored Iraq and Iran, including a remote set of mountains in Luristan.

Freya Stark, photographed in 1942

Freya wrote books about her travels and used the money she made from them to fund further trips and adventures. During World War II, Freya used her extensive knowledge of Arabia to help the British government with their military campaigns.

At the age of 76, Freya drove across Afghanistan in a jeep and camped at 2740m (9000ft) in the Himalayas, despite suffering from ill health. Aged 83, she sailed down the River Euphrates and at 86, she went pony-trekking in Nepal.

ALL AT SEA

There is an old superstition among sailors that women at sea bring bad luck. Despite this, many women have proved their seafaring skills. Some faced the sea alone; others managed to survive among hundreds of men aboard war and pirate ships.

Aboard a pirate ship

Anne Bonney left her home in Ireland for New Providence, one of a group of islands off the American coast now called the Bahamas. There she fell in love with John Rackham, a pirate captain also known as "Calico Jack".

Anne Bonney and Rackham's pirate flag

Anne helped Rackham steal the fastest ship in the local port. Together, they began a ten-year spree of piracy around the Caribbean.

Rackham often took sailors from other vessels to serve in his crew. Once, Anne found that a "young boy" who had been recruited in this way was actually a woman named Mary Read (1690-1720). Mary told Anne her story.

Mary Read

Mary Read began to dress like a man at an early age to increase her opportunities. She served as a cabin boy on a warship.

As an infantry soldier, she fought against Spain and France. She married a soldier who saw through her disguise.

When her husband died, Mary dressed as a man again and joined a ship. This ship was captured by John Rackham.

Anne Bonney and Mary Read became known all over the Caribbean as ferocious pirates. In 1720, Rackham's ship was finally captured by the British Navy off the coast of Jamaica. The two women fought fiercely with pistols, cutlasses and axes, even after the rest of the crew had surrendered.

Rackham and the crew were sentenced to death by hanging. Anne and Mary, however, couldn't be executed as they both claimed to be pregnant. They were released from their cells and disappeared. After that, nobody knows what happened to them. They were never heard of again.

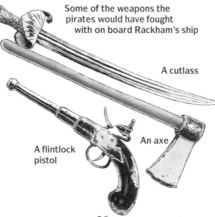

Some of the weapons the pirates would have fought with on board Rackham's ship

A cutlass

A flintlock pistol

An axe

Amazing Grace

On October 7, 1838, a steamship named the *Forfarshire* was dashed against rocks off the coast of Northumberland, England. From the nearby Longstone Lighthouse, Grace Darling (1815-42), the lighthouse keeper's daughter, spotted survivors in the water.

Grace and her father rowed to the rescue across rough seas. On their first trip they managed to pick up five survivors, two of whom helped them go back to the ship to rescue four more men.

The position of the wreck is marked with a cross. The route the Darlings rowed is shown in red.

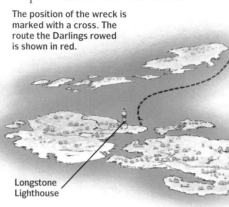

Longstone Lighthouse

Newspaper stories paid tribute to Grace Darling's heroism. Her part in the rescue was even recreated in a theatrical version of the wreck of the *Forfarshire*.

Unfortunately, the pressure of the publicity damaged Grace's health. Four years later she died, aged only 27.

A marble bust of Grace Darling

Over a period of 48 years, Ida Lewis (1842-1911), daughter of an American light-house keeper, rescued over a dozen sailors from shipwrecks around Lime Rock, off Newport, Rhode Island. Ida, however, enjoyed being a public heroine and she became the lighthouse keeper when her father retired.

Across the Channel

The first woman to swim the English Channel, the stretch of water between England and France, was a young American named Gertrude Ederle (b.1906). She was an international swimming champion who had won several Olympic medals and broken numerous world records.

To protect herself against the chilly waters of the Channel, Gertrude was smeared with grease.

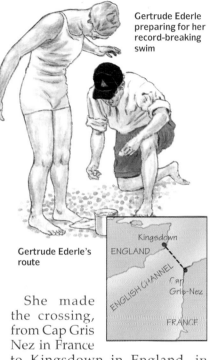

Gertrude Ederle preparing for her record-breaking swim

Gertrude Ederle's route

ENGLAND
Kingsdown

ENGLISH CHANNEL

Cap Gris-Nez

FRANCE

She made the crossing, from Cap Gris Nez in France to Kingsdown in England, in August 1926. It took her 14 hours and 39 minutes. This was nearly two hours less than the previous fastest crossing time.

Since Gertrude Ederle's record-breaking swim, many other women have conquered the Channel, including a 12-year-old girl and a pair of twin sisters.

Solo achievement

In 1977, New Zealander Naomi James (b.1949) began her attempt to become the first woman to sail single-handed around the world. She set sail in her yacht, the *Express Crusader*, from the port of Dartmouth in England. Her kitten, Boris, was her only companion for the 48,000km (30,000 mile) journey.

Despite having very little sailing experience, Naomi managed to cope with a broken radio, a cracked mast, and several other near-disasters, before successfully completing the historic journey. Her voyage lasted 272 days and broke the record for the fastest ever round-the-world yacht trip.

In recognition of her achievement, Naomi James was made a Dame of the British Empire.

This picture of the *Express Crusader* has been cut away to show the main living areas.

Naomi James on her boat, the *Express Crusader*.

Life raft

Every available space is designed to be used. This is for food storage.

Sleeping bunk

The radio was Naomi's only link with the rest of the world.

All the navigation calculations were carried out on this table.

The wheel, used to steer the yacht

AVIATORS AND ASTRONAUTS

Since the 1780s, when hot-air balloons first carried human passengers, women have been proving themselves excellent aviators. The most famous female flyers have made solo trips, showing amazing stamina and determination.

Up, up and away

The first balloons were flown in France, and the first women to fly in them were four French aristocrats. In May 1784, the Comtesse de Montalembert went up in a balloon, accompanied by three friends. However, this was not a real "flight", as the balloon was tied to the ground by a rope.

Only a fortnight later, Madame Thible became the first woman to pilot an untethered balloon, soaring to a height of 2,789m (8,500ft). Thrilled by her experience, she burst into song in mid-flight.

Dolly Shepherd, an early British stuntwoman, parachuting from a balloon wearing gold-trimmed knickerbockers

Early aviators

In 1908, over a century after her four ballooning countrywomen had made history, Madame Thérèse Peltier became the first woman to fly solo in a powered aircraft. It was another Frenchwoman, Baronne Raymonde de Laroche, who became the first qualified female pilot in 1910.

Raymonde de Laroche was given pilot's licence number 35.

Transatlantic triumph

Amelia Earhart (1898-1937), a social worker from Kansas, USA, was determined to become the first female pilot to fly across the Atlantic Ocean. She had already made the journey as a passenger, but she wanted to fly herself.

First, Amelia had extra fuel tanks, a new engine and navigational equipment added to her Vega aircraft.

She took off from Newfoundland on May 20, 1932. During the flight, she sipped tomato juice through a straw.

15 hours later, she landed safely in Ireland, in a field full of startled cows.

Amelia Earhart's famous transatlantic flight wasn't just the first by a female pilot. It was also quicker than any previous crossing. She went on to make many more adventurous long-distance flights.

In March 1937, she set out to fly around the world. But on the 2nd of July, toward the end of the trip, her plane ran out of fuel in the mid-Pacific. Amelia was never seen again.

This is a Lockheed Vega monoplane, similar to the one Amelia piloted on her record-breaking transatlantic flight.

Amy, Wonderful Amy

By spending most of the money that she earned on flying lessons, an English secretary named Amy Johnson (1903-41) fulfilled her ambition to become a qualified pilot and flight engineer. She then announced her intention to fly solo from England to Australia.

Amy took off from an airfield near London in her Gipsy Moth plane, *Jason*, on the morning of May 5, 1930. Over the next 19 days, she covered 16,000km (10,000 miles), landing to refuel at various airstrips on her flight path.

This is *Jason*, the bottle-green DH 60G Gipsy Moth plane in which Amy Johnson flew halfway across the world.

Amy had to repair *Jason*'s fragile structure several times during her historic journey.

In Burma, the broken wing of Amy's plane was patched using shirts donated by local people.

Extreme weather, desert sand-storms, choking fumes and only three hours sleep each night, all made Johnson's journey completely exhausting.

Unfortunately, a delay caused by a crash landing in Burma prevented Amy from reaching Australia in record time.

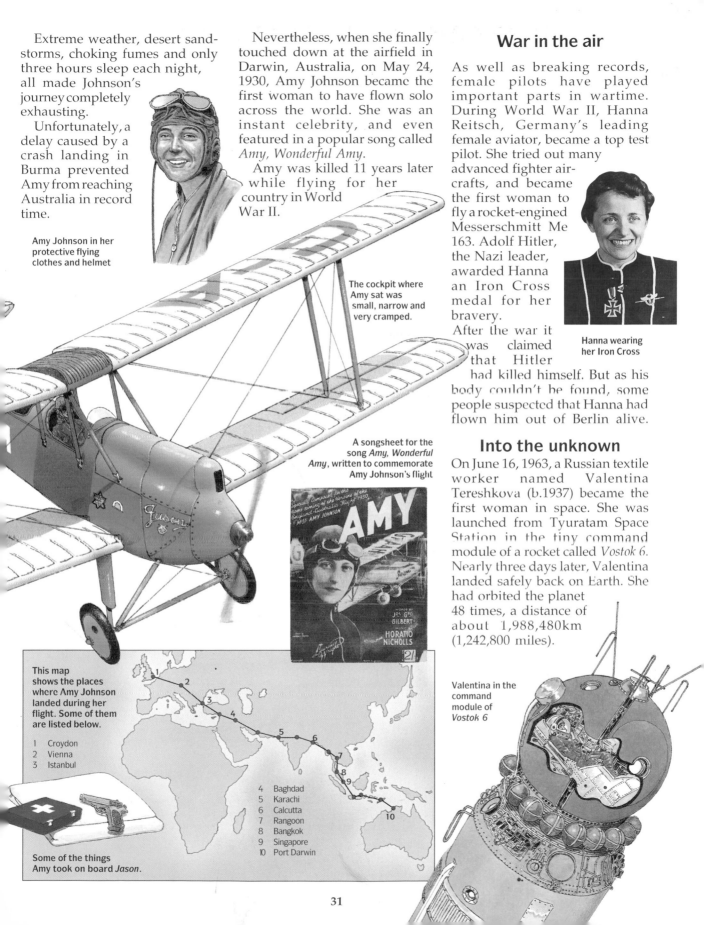

Amy Johnson in her protective flying clothes and helmet

Nevertheless, when she finally touched down at the airfield in Darwin, Australia, on May 24, 1930, Amy Johnson became the first woman to have flown solo across the world. She was an instant celebrity, and even featured in a popular song called *Amy, Wonderful Amy*.

Amy was killed 11 years later while flying for her country in World War II.

The cockpit where Amy sat was small, narrow and very cramped.

A songsheet for the song *Amy, Wonderful Amy*, written to commemorate Amy Johnson's flight

War in the air

As well as breaking records, female pilots have played important parts in wartime. During World War II, Hanna Reitsch, Germany's leading female aviator, became a top test pilot. She tried out many advanced fighter air-crafts, and became the first woman to fly a rocket-engined Messerschmitt Me 163. Adolf Hitler, the Nazi leader, awarded Hanna an Iron Cross medal for her bravery.

After the war it was claimed that Hitler had killed himself. But as his body couldn't be found, some people suspected that Hanna had flown him out of Berlin alive.

Hanna wearing her Iron Cross

Into the unknown

On June 16, 1963, a Russian textile worker named Valentina Tereshkova (b.1937) became the first woman in space. She was launched from Tyuratam Space Station in the tiny command module of a rocket called *Vostok 6*. Nearly three days later, Valentina landed safely back on Earth. She had orbited the planet 48 times, a distance of about 1,988,480km (1,242,800 miles).

Valentina in the command module of *Vostok 6*

This map shows the places where Amy Johnson landed during her flight. Some of them are listed below.

1 Croydon
2 Vienna
3 Istanbul

4 Baghdad
5 Karachi
6 Calcutta
7 Rangoon
8 Bangkok
9 Singapore
10 Port Darwin

Some of the things Amy took on board *Jason*.

LEADING LADIES

The ability to sing, dance and act has enabled many women to rise to fame. Performing is one area where leading ladies have succeeded in becoming the stars of the show.

Clara Schumann

From an early age, Clara Wieck (1819-96) displayed exceptional musical talent. She was performing professional piano recitals by the age of nine, and went on to become a composer of classical music and a great classical pianist.

At the age of 20, Clara married the composer Robert Schumann. She played many of his pieces and her tips and suggestions helped him achieve fame and recognition.

A piece of Robert Schumann's manuscript

After her husband's death in 1856, Clara became a successful music teacher. She helped many young musicians, including Johannes Brahms. She is said to have died while listening to her husband's piece *Intermezzi* being played by her grandson.

Clara Schumann at the piano

The divine Sarah

A French woman named Sarah Bernhardt (c.1844-1923) became one of the most famous stage actresses of the 19th century.

This picture shows Sarah Bernhardt in performance. She had a commanding stage presence.

Sarah toured the world, earning fame for her expressive acting and extravagant lifestyle. Her audiences never guessed that she suffered terribly from stage fright. She played hundreds of leading roles, including male ones, such as Hamlet.

Sarah became one of France's first film stars, but she always preferred the stage. She played many great roles in a theatre named after her, the Theatre-Sarah-Bernhardt in Paris.

Sarah worked right up to her death. She even went on stage with a wooden leg, after hers had been amputated.

Little Sure Shot

Annie Oakley (1860-1926), was the world's most famous trick shooter. As a child in her home state of Ohio, Annie helped her family pay their debts by shooting animals for sale at the market. By the age of 12, she had become a crack shot. She was later known as "Little Sure Shot".

In 1876, Annie married a marksman named Frank E. Butler, after beating him in a shooting match.

They developed a stage act in which Annie shot bullet holes through playing cards thrown in the air.

Annie's shooting skills impressed the crowds and earned her and her husband a living.

In 1885, Annie and Frank joined the Buffalo Bill Wild West Show and went touring all over the United States, along with several other performers. Annie soon had top billing in the show, and she soon became well-known throughout America. Later, Annie Oakley's life was turned into a musical called *Annie Get Your Gun*.

A poster advertising Annie and the Buffalo Bill Wild West Show

Dancing queen

The Russian dancer Anna Pavlova (1881-1931) was probably the most famous ballerina of all time.

When Anna was a girl, she was taken to see a famous ballet called *The Sleeping Beauty*. From that day, she decided that she wanted to be a ballet dancer.

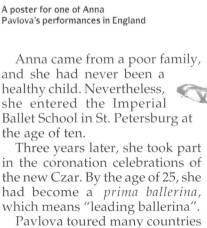

A poster for one of Anna Pavlova's performances in England

Anna came from a poor family, and she had never been a healthy child. Nevertheless, she entered the Imperial Ballet School in St. Petersburg at the age of ten.

Three years later, she took part in the coronation celebrations of the new Czar. By the age of 25, she had become a *prima ballerina*, which means "leading ballerina".

Pavlova toured many countries with the Imperial Ballet. Later, she set up her own ballet company and gave over 3,000 performances.

Many people in remote parts of the world were introduced to classical ballet through Anna's dancing. Audiences adored her graceful interpretation of solo parts such as the heroine in *Giselle*. She was so popular that when she went to Denmark, ballet fans pulled her carriage through the streets themselves.

One of Anna Pavlova's most famous roles was in a ballet called *Les Sylphides*. A leading Russian choreographer (dance arranger) named Mikhail Fokine created a solo dance especially for Pavlova, called *The Dying Swan*.

Anna died of pneumonia at the age of 49. She was worn out by two and a half decades of touring the world. Today, Anna Pavlova's name is also famous because a kind of meringue pie was named after her - perhaps because the shape of the pie looked like her ballet skirts.

These pictures of Anna Pavlova show three different moments in the ballet *Coppélia*.

Anna Pavlova played the role of Swanhilda in *Coppélia*, a story about a doll who comes to life.

Maria Callas

Maria Callas (1923-77) became one of the most famous dramatic sopranos of the 20th century. She was born in New York of Greek parents, and went to Greece when she was 14 years old to study music at the Athens Conservatory.

La Scala opera house in Milan

In 1947, Maria was asked to sing in an opera called *La Giaconda*. She gave a magnificent performance which launched her career. Over the next twenty years, she sang in many of the greatest opera houses in the world.

Maria was particularly acclaimed for the combination of her amazing voice and brilliant acting ability. She dominated the world of opera in the 1950s and 1960s.

Maria Callas on stage

Maria's dramatic private life added to her fame. She had a relationship with Aristotle Onassis, one of the world's richest men.

After retiring from the stage, Maria trained opera singers in New York.

WOMEN AND WORDS

Throughout history, women have excelled at writing, becoming highly respected authors. This may be because they could write even when confined to their homes.

Sappho

The Greek poet Sappho lived on the island of Lesbos and wrote during the 6th century BC. Only 650 lines of her poetry, and only one complete poem, have survived.

Sappho led a group of women who gave worship to Aphrodite, the goddess of love. Many of her poems are about women and love.

Sappho shown on an ancient Greek vase

Little is known about Sappho's life, except what we know from her own poetry and from comic dramas written about her. She and her husband, Cercylas, had three sons and a daughter. One story about Sappho tells of her love for a man named Phaon, and how she committed suicide by throwing herself from a cliff.

Sappho's influence on other poets who copied her style shows that she was an important writer at a time when women rarely achieved recognition. She is best known for her lyric verse, a kind of songlike poetry.

Love letters

When she was widowed at the age of 25, Christine de Pisan (1364-1430) was left with her children, her mother and brothers to support. She became probably the first woman to earn her living through writing. At the court of Charles V of France she found many patrons (wealthy supporters) to pay for her writing.

Christine de Pisan

Christine produced a huge amount of work. She wrote about "courtly love", the medieval system in which men swore loyalty and devotion to the women they loved. She also wrote essays that encouraged women to educate themselves.

After a full career as a writer, Christine retired to a convent in 1418. She lived long enough however, to write a tribute to Jeanne d'Arc (see page 9) whom she saw as a model of feminine courage.

Many courtly love poems described tournaments at which knights jousted.

The women watch from their tent.

Pen names

In some countries, writing used to be considered an unsuitable profession for women. As a result, many female poets and novelists published their work under false male names, or "pen names".

The Brontës were three English sisters named Charlotte (1816-55), Emily (1818-48), and Anne (1820-49). They first found literary fame under the pen names of Currer, Ellis, and Acton Bell (keeping their real initials).

A portrait of Charlotte, the eldest of the Brontë sisters

Some female writers found it easier to live as a man as well. One French authoress named Amandine Aurore Lucie Dupin (1804-1876) published more than 40 novels under the pen name George Sand. She also frequently dressed in men's clothes, to enjoy the increased social freedom they allowed her.

Knights fought on horseback, each carrying the banner of the lady he wanted to impress.

A hidden talent

In the 1930s, the Nazis, a political party in power in Germany, began to terrorize the Jewish population. Otto Frank, a Jewish businessman, took his family to Amsterdam in the Netherlands to escape persecution. But in 1941, the Germans invaded the Netherlands, and the Frank family were in danger.

The Franks and another Jewish family called the van Daans went into hiding in a secret apartment at Otto's warehouse. For two years they avoided detection, relying on friends outside to bring them supplies and news.

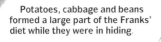

A page from Anne's diary

Potatoes, cabbage and beans formed a large part of the Franks' diet while they were in hiding.

Throughout the ordeal, Otto's youngest daughter Anne (1929-45) kept a diary, recording the daily life of the family in hiding. She wrote it in the form of letters to an imaginary friend named "Kitty". The diary relates the difficulties the Frank family faced.

The building in this picture has been cut away to show the secret attic where the Franks and the van Daans lived in hiding.

A photo of Anne Frank

Anne described how they were almost discovered when the building was sold and an architect came to look at it. Another time, the warehouse was searched by police after a burglary.

Tragically, the Franks were discovered by the Nazi police a few months before the end of the war, and were sent to concentration camps. Only Otto Frank survived. He published Anne's diary after the war. Its translation into more than 30 languages has made Anne Frank a worldwide symbol of wartime suffering and courage.

Anne wrote most of her diary in this attic room.

The beds were put away during the day to make space.

Secret entrance

The entrance to the attic was hidden behind furniture in the main part of the building.

The lower part of the building was a warehouse.

Maya Angelou

In 1970, Maya Angelou (b.1928) became the first African-American woman to have a non-fiction book in the bestseller lists. It was the first volume of her autobiography and was called *I Know Why the Caged Bird Sings*.

Maya Angelou

The book told of Maya's childhood in Arkansas in the 1930s. She grew up in a rural town called Stamps, where the black and white communities were strongly divided. At the age of eight, she was abused by her mother's boyfriend. When he was murdered, she blamed herself and didn't speak for five years.

Before turning to writing, Maya was an actress, a singer, a dancer and a cook. She also worked with civil rights leaders such as Martin Luther King and Malcolm X, who fought for equal rights for black people in America.

As well as her autobiographical books, Maya Angelou has published several volumes of poetry. She is one of America's leading poets, and was invited to read a poem at the 1993 ceremony at which Bill Clinton was made President of the USA.

CREATIVE GENIUS

There have been far fewer famous women artists than women writers. This may be because, in the past, the cost of being an artist was beyond many women. Now, however, the number of female visual artists is increasing.

An independent spirit

Today, the talents of the Italian-born figure painter Artemisia Gentileschi (1593-c.1651) are highly respected. From an early age, Artemisia was encouraged to paint by her father, who was himself a successful painter.

Artemisia is best known for her paintings of women in scenes from history, myths or the Bible. Her most famous work is called *Judith and Holofernes*. It shows the Jewish heroine Judith cutting off the head of Holofernes, who was an enemy of her people.

Artemisia became famous throughout Italy for her skill. She learned to stand up for herself and negotiated good prices for her paintings.

Some people think that Artemisia's determination to be a truly independent woman came from an incident that happened when she was only 18.

In 1612, Artemisia's father accused a man of raping his daughter and stealing some paintings.

The accused was a man named Tassi, Artemisia's painting teacher. She gave evidence against him, but he was set free.

After the trial, Artemisia went on painting. Her experience may have influenced her choice of subject matter.

Lights, camera, action!

Leni Riefenstahl was born in Berlin, Germany in 1902. She started her career as a dancer. After appearing in several films, Leni began to direct her own films and founded her own film company.

The dancer and film-maker Leni Reifenstahl

Leni Riefenstahl has been criticised for her association with Adolf Hitler, the leader of a political party called the Nazis who came to power in the 1930s. At Hitler's request, she wrote and produced a film called *Triumph of Will*, which shows a Nazi rally at Nuremberg. Technically it is a masterpiece, with its brilliant camera angles, moving shots and clever editing. But the film appears to glorify Hitler and his supporters.

Hitler provided money for Leni's film *Olympia*, a documentary about the 1936 Olympic Games in Berlin. When the film was finished, however, she refused an order from the Nazi party to remove scenes showing the black American athelete, Jesse Owens, who won four gold medals at the competition.

After World War II, Leni was put on a blacklist of artists who had been associated with the Nazis. She was refused work, and did not make another film until 1957.

Barbara Hepworth

Barbara Hepworth (1903-1975) knew she wanted to sculpt even when she was a child. She became one of the most influential sculptors of the 20th century.

Barbara studied art in London and Italy, and was one of the first great creators of abstract sculptures. Instead of portraying objects or people in a realistic fashion, her sculptures used lines, textures and shapes to convey emotions and moods.

Barbara worked in wood, metal and stone. She claimed that she always knew what the final shape of a sculpture would be before she began.

Orpheus (1956). The curving shapes of this sculpture are typical of Barbara's graceful style.

She often worked until her arms ached and her fingers were bruised and bleeding.

In 1939, Barbara moved to Cornwall, in southwest England, where she became influenced by the landscape, the sea and the sky and local ancient monuments.

Barbara Hepworth's most famous work was a large sculpture for the Dag Hammarskjöld memorial at the United Nations Building in New York. She was still working when she died, aged 72, in a fire in her studio in Cornwall in 1975.

Good vibrations

The British painter Bridget Riley (b.1931) became one of the world's leading abstract artists. She was fascinated by the patterns and vibrations she saw in nature. This led her to develop a new style of art known as Optical art, or Op art.

In the 1960s, Bridget painted striking black and white pictures which play tricks on the eye and appear to move and shimmer. Her style had an important influence on other artists and on the design world. Op art dresses with striking black and white patterns became very fashionable.

On a trip to Egypt in 1981, Bridget was inspired to use the shades chosen by ancient Egyptian artists, bringing a new intensity and light to her pictures.

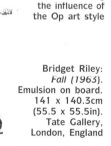

A 1960s dress, showing the influence of the Op art style

Bridget Riley: *Fall* (1963). Emulsion on board. 141 x 140.3cm (55.5 x 55.5in). Tate Gallery, London, England

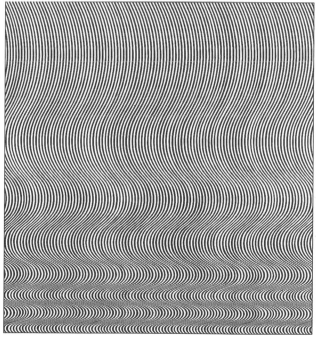

Paula Rego's painting *The Maids*, based on a 20th-century play about a murder.

A fairytale artist

Born in Portugal in 1935, Paula Rego became an internationally renowned painter, illustrator and printmaker.

At sixteen, she was sent to a school in England by her father, but left the school after a few months to attend art school in London.

Paula's early work in the 1960s consisted of collages, made by sticking pieces of paper together to make pictures.

Many of her pictures are based on the traditional fairy tales she heard as a child in Portugal. In her work, art is often used as another way to tell stories.

Like the fairy tales that inspired her paintings, her work can often be sinister and frightening. The idea for her picture *The Maids* is taken from a play by the 20th century French writer Jean Genet, in which a group of maids murder their mistress.

In 1990, Paula Rego became the first woman to be appointed an Associate Artist at the National Gallery in London. Working from a studio in the Gallery, she completed a large wall painting. The wall painting tells the stories of female saints and courageous women.

Little Miss Muffet, like many of Paula Rego's works, is based on a traditional tale.

SCIENTIFIC MINDS

Throughout history, women have been involved in the development of science and medicine, but their achievements have often gained little recognition. For centuries, women were unable to attend universities and were excluded from scientific societies and laboratories. Even today, there are far fewer women working in the sciences than men.

Tombstone of a woman doctor from the 1st century AD

Caroline Herschel

Caroline compiled lists of the stars and comets they observed. She became the first woman to be appointed assistant to the Court Astronomer. As well as her work for her brother, Caroline discovered eight new comets herself. She won several awards for her findings and, in 1835, she and another scientist, Mary Somerville, became the first women to be awarded honorary memberships of the Royal Astronomical Society.

Star gazer

In 1772, Caroline Herschel (1750-1848) left Germany and went to England to work with her brother William, an astronomer. She taught herself astronomy and mathematics so that she could assist her brother with his studies.

Together they built a giant telescope and used it to study the night sky.

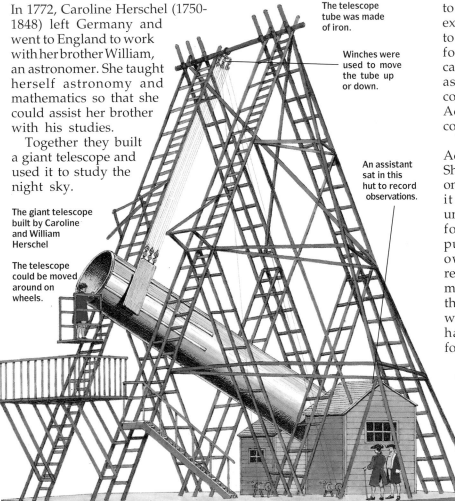

The giant telescope built by Caroline and William Herschel

The telescope could be moved around on wheels.

The telescope tube was made of iron.

Winches were used to move the tube up or down.

An assistant sat in this hut to record observations.

Computer Countess

Ada, Countess of Lovelace (1815-52), was the daughter of Lord Byron, a well-known English poet. At the age of 18, she attended a lecture and saw an early calculating machine built by a famous mathematician named Charles Babbage.

Babbage's machine, known as the Analytical Engine

Ada was fascinated. She began to work with Babbage, using her exceptional mathematical ability to design arithmetical operations for the new machines. These calculating machines are now seen as the forerunners of modern computers. So, in a sense, Ada was the first ever computer programmer.

Babbage encouraged Ada to publish her work. She signed her work with only her initials, because it was considered unsuitable at that time for a woman to publish under her own name. As a result, her work as a mathematician, like that of many other women scientists, has largely been forgotten.

A portrait of Ada, Countess of Lovelace

In addition to working with Babbage, Ada conducted several other mathematical investigations. She even spent time trying to develop a fool-proof gambling system. Her work was cut short when she died in 1852, at the age of only 37.

Marie Curie

Polish-born Marie Sklodowska (1867-1934) was the first world-famous female scientist. She studied physics at the Sorbonne University in Paris. She worked long hours and could hardly afford to eat.

In 1895, she married Pierre Curie and together they began to research materials which gave out radiation. They discovered two new substances, which they called polonium and radium, that emitted high levels of radiation.

In 1903, the Curies won a Nobel prize for physics. Marie was the first woman to receive this award.

A medal showing a bust of Marie Curie

Two years later, Pierre Curie was killed in a road accident. Marie took over his position as professor in Paris, becoming the first woman professor in France. In 1911, she won a second Nobel prize, this time for chemistry.

Radium in small doses became very important in the treatment of cancer. But years of exposure to it had damaged Marie's own health. She died of a blood cancer in 1934.

Marie in the shed that was her laboratory

A model scientist

In 1951, English scientist Rosalind Franklin (1920-58) began studying a chemical called deoxyribonucleic acid (DNA). Scientists thought DNA acted as a chemical code of instructions that decided what characteristics an animal inherited from its parents.

Rosalind took part in a race between scientists to explain the structure of DNA. She and one of her colleagues, Maurice Wilkins, studied it using X-ray photographs.

They were beaten by two other scientists, Crick and Watson (both men), who built a model of a DNA molecule. Crick and Watson were accused of using the results of Rosalind Franklin's research to produce their model.

In 1962, Crick, Watson and Wilkins were jointly awarded the Nobel prize for medicine. Rosalind Franklin would have shared the prize, but she had died of cancer four years earlier, aged only 38.

The model of a DNA molecule looks a little like a twisted rope ladder.

Gene genius

When Barbara McClintock (b.1902) was a teenager, her parents discouraged her interest in science. They thought it was an unsuitable career for a girl. Eventually, however, she studied biology at Cornell University, USA.

Barbara McClintock

Barbara specialized in genetics, the science of heredity. She noticed that, in some cells, genes changed their position. This could cause other genes to stop functioning, with unexpected results. These genes were nick-named "jumping genes". In an African violet plant, for example, she observed that jumping genes caused pigment genes to stop working, causing a loss of pigment in some of the flower's petals.

This diagram shows how a gene "jumps".

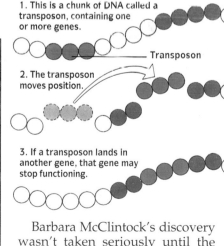

1. This is a chunk of DNA called a transposon, containing one or more genes.

Transposon

2. The transposon moves position.

3. If a transposon lands in another gene, that gene may stop functioning.

Barbara McClintock's discovery wasn't taken seriously until the 1970s, when advances in molecular biology revealed that she had been right. In 1983, she received a Nobel prize for her work.

GREAT BUSINESSWOMEN

Big business has often excluded women from top jobs. Yet women have used new ideas, and their understanding of what other women want, to succeed in business.

Seeds of success

In the 18th century, one of the main industries in the southern states of America was growing, harvesting and processing cotton. Separating the seeds of a cotton plant from the fluffy part known as the boll, was a very slow process done by hand.

A head of cotton

In 1793, a man named Eli Whitney invented a machine known as the "cotton gin", which could separate the cotton from its seeds much faster than before. The idea was turned into a business success by Catherine Greene (1755-1814), the widow of a wealthy plantation owner.

A model of the cotton gin

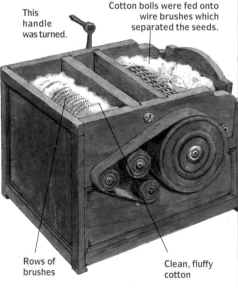

This handle was turned.

Cotton bolls were fed onto wire brushes which separated the seeds.

Rows of brushes

Clean, fluffy cotton

Catherine realized that Eli Whitney's invention would revolutionize the cotton trade. She put her money into developing and publicizing the idea. The gin was so successful that it made her a vast fortune.

Fantastic wax

Swiss-born Philippe Curtius made his fortune sculpting portraits in wax. His wax museum in Paris, the *Cabinet de cire*, became a major public attraction.

Curtius taught his niece, Marie Tussaud (1761-1850), the skills of working with wax. She quickly became very good at making models, and her portraits of the famous people of her day helped to increase the museum's success. In 1774, Philippe Curtius died and Madame Tussaud, as Marie became known, inherited and took over the museum.

A wax model of Madame Tussaud making a head in her workroom

This self-portrait was the last model that Madame Tussaud ever made.

By 1802, Marie was having financial problems. She decided to seek her fortune overseas, and over the next 30 years, she toured the British Isles with her collection of life-size waxworks of rogues and heroes.

Marie was an excellent judge of what the public would pay to see, and continually added new models to her exhibition. Her waxworks were so successful in Britain that in 1835 she was able to set up a permanent exhibition, known as Madame Tussaud's, in London. Nearly 150 years after her death, the museum is still famous all over the world, and is one of London's main tourist attractions, with models of many modern celebrities.

A wax model of the Hollywood actor Mel Gibson, one of the modern exhibits at Madame Tussaud's

Champagne champion

When she was widowed at the age of 27, Nicole-Barbe Cliquot-Ponsardin (1777-1866) was determined to run her husband's wine-making business. Her father-in-law wanted to shut the company down, but Nicole-Barbe relaunched it with a new name, Veuve Cliquot and Company (*Veuve Cliquot* means "Widow Cliquot" in French).

Nicole-Barbe developed a way of removing unwanted waste from champagne, known as *la méthode champenoise*. It is still used today, over a century later.

A bottle is placed in a specially designed rack, which tips it gently so that the sediment sinks to the bottom.

The angle at which the bottle is tipped is slowly increased until the sediment rests on top of the cork.

The cork and the sediment are removed and a new cork is put in. None of the gas that makes the wine fizzy is lost.

Nicole-Barbe's business talents ensured that her firm's trade soared. She earned a personal fortune and a lasting reputation as a shrewd business woman.

Chanel

Gabrielle Chanel (1883-1971), known as Coco, was the daughter of a French peasant family. She was orphaned at a young age and began working with her sister, making hats.

The stylish Coco Chanel wearing one of her own designs

During World War I, Coco served as a nurse. But when the war was over, she borrowed money from an English lover and set up a dress shop in her hometown of Deauville.

The shop's popularity allowed Coco to transfer her business to Paris, where she opened another shop. Her designing talent sparked an international fashion revolution.

The secret of Coco's success was that she created clothes that were simple and comfortable, yet very elegant and glamorous. Designs such as the "little black dress" and the Chanel collarless suit soon became very popular.

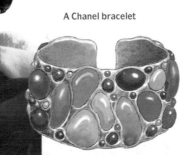

This elegant suit was designed in the 1960s and is typical of the Chanel style.

Before long, Coco dominated the fashion trade. The success of her perfume, *Chanel No. 5*, made her a millionairess. She led a dazzling social life and was often written about in newspapers.

By 1938, however, new styles were competing with hers, and Coco decided to retire. But in 1954, she staged a successful comeback, quickly regaining her status in the fashion world. She relaunched her original designs, which soon proved to be as popular as ever.

A Chanel bracelet

Natural woman

While she was visiting South America, Anita Roddick (b.1943) noticed how local women cared for their skin and hair using traditional, natural methods. When she returned to England, she opened a small shop called The Body Shop, selling cosmetics based on natural products.

Anita Roddick (left) learning about beauty treatments from the Ñahñu Indians

To keep costs down and reduce unnecessary waste, Anita packaged her beauty products in cheap plastic containers, and encouraged her customers to bring them back to be refilled.

Today there are nearly 1,400 branches of The Body Shop in 45 countries throughout the world. The company is dedicated to a policy of environmentally friendly business practices, and their products aren't tested on animals. The company also stresses the importance of trading fairly with developing countries. Through The Body Shop, Anita Roddick has become one of Britain's most successful businesswomen.

One of The Body Shop's 1,400 premises

SPORTING SUCCESS

The women of ancient Greece were not allowed to compete in the Olympic Games, which were held every four years in the city of Olympia. Instead, they set up their own sporting festival, the *Heraea*. Today, women not only take part in the·Olympics, but also compete professionally in a wide range of sports, from diving to darts.

Statue of a woman runner

The ice queen

The first female sports celebrity was probably Sonja Henie (1912-69) who was born in Norway. She became the national women's skating champion at the age of 11. She went on to win a gold medal for figure-skating in three consecutive Winter Olympics, in 1928, 1932 and 1936.

Sonja Henie competing at the 1932 Olympics

After her third Olympic victory, Sonja decided to become a paid performer in ice shows. Later, she changed from a sporting career to acting stardom, and made 11 Hollywood films. She was the first to wear the short skating skirts which are still worn by skaters today.

A true talent

Probably the most·versatile sportswoman of modern times was an American named Mildred Didrikson (1914-56). She excelled brilliantly in almost every sport she tried, from swimming, diving and skating, to tennis, baseball and billiards.

Babe, as she was known to her fans, began her sporting career at the age of 16, when she became a professional basketball player. At the same age, she won medals for swimming, and broke athletics records in every track and field event she entered.

During the 1932 Oympics in Los Angeles, Babe was cheered to victory by her home crowd. She won an incredible six medals, in events ranging from hurdling and high jumping to throwing the javelin. On one day, she broke four world records in only three hours.

In the 1940s, Babe went on to dominate yet another sport, becoming the world's top female golfer. In 1947, she won 17 successive golf tournaments.

Babe powering to victory in the women's 100m hurdles during the 1932 Olympic Games in Los Angeles

In 1953, Babe underwent major surgery for cancer, but the following year she still managed to win five major golf titles. Sadly her illness grew worse, and she died at the age of 42.

Babe completing a golfing swing

A controversial star

Australian-born Dawn Fraser (b.1937) was the first swimmer to win gold medals for the same event in three consecutive Olympics. The event was the 100m freestyle. During her career, she broke 27 world records. She estimated that she had swum a total of 16,000km (10,000 miles). Dawn became famous for her adventures both in and out of the pool.

Dawn was involved in a car crash. Tragically, her mother was killed and Dawn, who was driving, was badly injured.

In the 1960 Olympics, Dawn refused to swim in the medley relay, so she was dropped from the Australian team.

At the 1964 Games, Dawn stole a flag and a policeman's bike. She was banned from competing for ten years.

Perfect gymnasts

During the 1972 Munich Olympics, a tiny Soviet gymnast named Olga Korbut (b.1956) delighted crowds with her personality and performances. She won two individual gold medals and helped the Soviet squad win a gold team medal. Her trademark was a daring back flip in her beam routine.

Olga's dazzling displays had a huge effect on the worldwide popularity of gymnastics.

The gold medals won by Olga Korbut in the 1972 Games

Olga Korbut performing a back flip at the 1972 Olympics. The beam measures 10cm (4 inches) wide.

| Olga swings her arms upward as she jumps. | She pulls her knees up to her chest to start turning. | She begins to untuck her legs to stop turning. | She lands firmly, with both feet on the beam. | She maintains her balance as she begins to stand. | She ends in a perfect finishing position. |

Within months of Olga's success, many young people were inspired to take up the sport. Membership numbers of amateur clubs shot up worldwide.

In the 1976 Montreal Olympics, another young gymnast stole the limelight. Fourteen-year-old Nadia Comaneci (b.1961) of Romania became the first gymnast to achieve a perfect score of 10 out of 10. She received this score seven times, winning three individual gold medals and a team silver medal. Her most famous move was a dismount from the asymmetric bars, involving a twisting back flip.

Nadia performing her beam routine at the 1976 Olympic Games at Montreal, Canada

Number one

Martina Navratilova (b. 1956) was trained to be a world champion by her tennis-loving stepfather.

At the age of 19, Martina secretly left Czechoslovakia, after repeated arguments with the national tennis authorities, to live in America. In 1975, she became a professional player, and over the next two decades she won 167 titles and was ranked world number one for 332 weeks. By the end of 1994, she had won over $20 million in prize money.

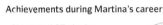

Achievements during Martina's career

- She won 167 singles titles, more than any other player.

- She won 165 doubles titles.

- She won 19 titles at Wimbledon, having played there for 23 years.

- Between January and December 1984, she set the longest consecutive match winning streak, at 74 matches.

- She was ranked No.1 player in the world for 332 weeks.

- She was named Female Athlete of the Decade in the 1980s.

- In 1991, she became the oldest female finalist in U.S. Open history.

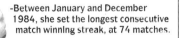

Martina Navratilova demonstrating the amazing strength and speed which made her a world champion

MEDIA STARS

Mass media, such as television, radio, film and the press, have been responsible for a greater, more widespread kind of fame. Some women have almost become famous for being famous.

A silent star

The first woman to dominate the movie world was American actress Mary Pickford (1893-1979). She began to act in touring shows at only five years old. She appeared in her first movie in 1909, when she was paid $5 a week to play a small role in *The Violin Maker of Cremona*.

Mary Pickford

Her acting ability and beauty soon brought her great success. She planned her movie career with care and determination. Her many

In silent movies, the actors used gestures to show their feelings.

Cameras like these were used to shoot silent films.

Mary Pickford made over 200 silent movies.

successful films included *Rebecca of Sunnybrook Farm* (1917) and *Poor Little Rich Girl* (1917).

In 1916, she formed a film company which later became United Artists, one of the movie industry's leading companies. Mary was well-known for her tough business mind and became one of the richest self-made women in America, earning about $1,000,000 a year. Her vast fortune was estimated at $50 million. She worked hard however, often for more than 15 hours a day. She made over 200 silent movies and four "talkies". She decided to retire at the age of 40 years old, while she was at her peak of her profession.

Marilyn Monroe

The most famous Hollywood screen star and one of the most famous faces in history is American film star Marilyn Monroe (1926-1962).

Marilyn, whose real name was Norma Jean Baker, spent much of her childhood in foster homes, because her mother suffered from mental illness. In 1946, she became a photographer's model, but she dreamed of being a star and went to Hollywood.

After a series of small parts and a lot of publicity from the film studio she worked for, she starred in a film called *Niagara* (1952). She went on to make *How to Marry a Millionaire* (1953).

In January 1954, she married Joe di Maggio who was an American baseball star and national hero. Together they entertained American troops fighting in Korea.

In 1956, Marilyn married Arthur Miller, a famous playwright.

Marilyn often played the part of the "dumb blonde".

She went on to make some of her best films, including *Bus Stop* (1956), *The Prince and the Showgirl* (1957), and *Some Like It Hot* (1959), a comedy.

Marilyn's health, however, began to decline as she grew increasingly addicted to alcohol and sleeping pills. Tragically, she died of a drug overdose in 1962.

Marilyn singing to entertain US troops in Korea in 1954

In full voice

Lata Mangeshkar was born in Indore, central India, in 1929. Her father, a well known singer and actor, taught her to sing classical Indian music from an early age. He died when Lata was thirteen and, as the eldest of five children, she became responsible for supporting the family.

She became a "playback singer". This means she provided the singing voice of actresses in Indian musical fims. At first, her voice was considered "too thin" and the first song she recorded was cut from the movie. A year later, however, she proved her critics wrong and rose to the top of her profession.

In a career lasting for over 50 years, she sang in more than 1600 films. She appeared in *The Guinness Book of Records* for having recorded more songs than anyone else in the world.

Lata Mangeshkar has performed to audiences all over the world, and has received many awards both in India and abroad. In 1979, she was the first Asian to receive a platinum disc for her international record sales.

A poster for an Indian musical film

Madonna

Pop music has become a huge industry, with a great influence over the lives and ideas of young people. It is one area in which women's success has come close to that of men. Pop stars like Madonna are among the most famous people in the world.

Madonna, whose full name is Madonna Louise Ciccone, was born in the USA in 1958. She studied dance at the University of Michigan, but left her studies to seek fame and fortune in New York. She began her career working as a backing singer and club dancer, but was determined to become a superstar.

Madonna performing in concert

She certainly succeeded. Her first album, *Madonna,* included five hit singles. She has also starred in films, including *Desperately Seeking Susan* (1985) and *Dick Tracy* (1990).

In 1990, her controversial Blonde Ambition Tour cost 4.5 million dollars to produce. It quickly became notorious for its raunchy dance routines and outrageous costumes by the French designer Jean-Paul Gaultier.

Supermodels

The term 'supermodel' was invented by the media in the late 1980s. It was used to describe models who become celebrities in their own right, more famous than the fashion houses they represented. Supermodels such as American Cindy Crawford and German Claudia Schiffer became household names.

Many supermodels have used their fame to expand their careers beyond the fashion catwalks. They host television shows, promote beauty products and star in films.

A typical example is Naomi Campbell (b.1970), who was discovered by a model agency at the age of 15 when she was out shopping in London. As well as being a model, she has written a novel and released a record.

Naomi Campbell on the catwalk

Naomi is known as the supermodel who is most successful at selling outfits to an audience.

A LIST OF FEMALE FIRSTS

BC

2700BC
Probably the first recorded medical practitioner was a woman named Merit Ptah (Egyptian).

1503BC
The only recorded woman Pharaoh was Hatshepsut (Egyptian), who seized power from her stepson and ruled as a "king".

43BC
The first woman to lead a march for women's rights was a Greek woman named Hortensia who protested against unfair taxes on women.

AD

c.497
The first recorded female social reformer was Empress Theodora of Byzantium. She opened a home to rehabilitate prostitutes.

855
A woman may have been elected Pope. The story goes that her true sex was only discovered when she gave birth to a child in the middle of a procession through the streets of Rome.

c.1300
The first known sculptress was Sabina von Steinbach (German), who carved figures in the Cathedral at Strasbourg, France.

1766
The first woman to sail around the world was Jeanne Baret (French). She made the journey disguised as a man, on a ship called the *Etoile*.

1784
The first woman to fly in a tethered balloon was the Comtesse de Montalembert (French).

1784
The first woman to fly in an untethered balloon was Madame Thible (French).

1850
The first woman to become a model was Marie Worth (French), who wore dresses designed by her husband Charles Worth.

1879
The first woman to plead before the American Supreme Court was Belva Lockwood (American).

1886
The birth of the first distinctive female Blues singer, Gertrude "Ma" Rainey (American).

1901
The first woman to pilot an airship solo was an actress named Aida d'Acosta (American).

1903
The first woman to receive a Nobel prize for physics was Marie Curie (Polish).

1905
The first woman to win a Nobel peace prize was Bertha von Suttner (Austrian). She is said to have persuaded Alfred Nobel to establish the peace prize.

1908
The first woman to set a world record for swimming was Martha Gerstung (German) for the 100m freestyle.

1909
The first woman to win a Nobel prize for literature was Selma Lagerlöf (Swedish), for her novel *Gösta Berlings*.

1909
The birth of Myra Logan (American), the first woman to operate on a human heart.

1917
The first woman to win a Pulitzer prize for biography was Laura Richards (American) for a book about her mother.

1919
The first woman pilot to fly across the Andes mountains in South America was Adrienne Bolland (French). She had to withstand severe cold and lack of oxygen.

1922
The first woman to win a Pulitzer prize for fiction was Willa Cather (American) for her novel entitled *One of Ours*.

1923
The first European woman to enter the city of Lhasa in Tibet was Alexandra David-Neel (French).

1926
The first woman to swim the English Channel was Gertrude Ederle (American).

1927
The first woman to appear in a "talkie" scene of a full-length movie was Eugenie Besserer, an American actress. The film was *The Jazz Singer*.

1928
The first woman to fly across the Atlantic was Amelia Earhart (American).

1930
The first woman to fly solo from London to Australia was Amy Johnson (British).

1930
The first female flight attendant was a nurse named Ellen Church (American).

1935
The first woman to become a sea-captain was Anna Schetinina (Soviet).

1936
The birth of Sarah Breedlove (American), the first self-made millionairess, who made her fortune from "hair straightener".

1943
The first female ambassador was Alexandra Kollontai (Soviet) who took a post in Sweden.

1947
The first woman to hold the position of foreign minister was Ana Pauker of Romania.

1952
The first woman to sail across the Atlantic single-handed was Anne Davison (British).

1953
The first woman to break the sound barrier was aviator Jacqueline Cochrane (American).

1956
The first swimmer to win the same title in three successive Olympic Games was Dawn Fraser (Australian). She was also the first woman to swim the 100m in under one minute.

1960
The first woman prime minister was Sirimavo Bandaranaike (Sri Lankan), who succeeded her husband.

1963
The first woman in space was Valentina Tereshkova (Soviet), who stayed in orbit for three days.

1966
Scientist Lise Meitner (Austrian) was the first woman to win a Fermi award. Her work proved that an atom could be split to release energy.

1968
The first African-American woman elected to the American Congress was Shirley Chisholm.

1969
The first woman to walk across the North Polar ice-cap was Myrtle Simpson (British). Unfortunately she failed in an attempt to reach the North Pole

1969
The first woman to sail single-handed across the Pacific Ocean from Yokohama, Japan to San Diego, USA, was Sharon Adams (American).

1971
The first woman to row across the Pacific Ocean in a rowing boat was Sylvia Cook (British).

1971
The first woman judge at the European Court of Human Rights was Helga Pederson (Danish).

1973
The first modern woman bull fighter was Angela Hernandez (Spanish).

1975
The first woman to reach the summit of Mount Everest was Junko Tabei (Japanese).

1975
The first woman to receive the American Institute of Chemists award, for her work in discovering an antibiotic that was effective against disease, was Rachel Brown (American)

1976
The first woman to sail successfully around the world single-handed was yachtswoman Krystyna Chojnowska Liskiewicz. (Polish). It took her two years.

1976
The first woman to achieve a perfect score (10 out of 10) in gymnastics was Nadia Comaneci (Romanian).

1978
The birth of Louise Brown (English) the world's first test-tube baby.

1980
The first woman to be elected head of state was Vigdís Finnbogadóttir (Icelandic) who became the President of Iceland.

1990
Benazir Bhutto, Prime Minister of Pakistan, became the first head of state to give birth to a child while in government.

1993
Toni Morrison became the first African-American woman to be awarded the Nobel prize for literature.

1994
The first woman to win the Palme D'Or (a French award for film-making) was Jane Campion (New Zealander), with her film *The Piano*.

INDEX

The publisher would like to thank the following organizations for permission to reproduce their material (l = left, r = right, t = top, b = bottom, tr = top right, bl = bottom left etc.): Allsport, 3(l), 42(l), 43(l); The Body Shop, UK, 41(tr, br), Ñahñu Indians / Antonio Vizcaino; The Brontë Society, 36; Camera Press, 35(l); Colorsport, 43(r); Corbis / Bettmann, 6(b), 15(t), 18, 39(l), 42(r), 44(tr,); Corbis / Bettmann / UPI, 7(b), 15(b), 17, 39(r), 44(br); Express Newspapers, 29; FDR Library, 25(t); Hulton Getty, cover(l, bl), 13, 14, 31(t), 44(l); Jane Addams Memorial Collection, Special Collections, The University Library, The University of Illinois at Chicago, 11(tl); Madame Tussaud's, London, 40; The Raymond Mander and Joe Mitchenson Theatre Collection, 33(l); The Maria Montessori Training Organization, AMI, London, England, 11(tr, b); Mary Evans Picture Library, cover(tl), 3(t), 31(b); MSI / Hulton Getty, (cover tr); Peter Newark's Western America, 32(b); Popperfoto, cover (r), 24, 32(t), 37(b), 41(tl); Prudence Cumings Associates, 35 (t, br) (The Maids / Saatchi Collection); Punch, 23(l); Rex Features Ltd, 6(t), 7(r), 23(r), 25(r), 37(t), 41(bl), 45(t, br); Royal Geographical Society, London, 27, courtesy The Freya Stark Estate; Tate Galley, London, 34(r) (Orpheus 1956 © Alan Bowness, Hepworth Estate), 35(bl); Tony Stone Images, 3(r); Topham, 25(b), 34(l); Wallace Collection, London / Bridgeman Art Library, London, 5; Zoë Dominic, 33(r).

First published in 1996 by Usborne Publishing Ltd, Usborne House, 83-85 Saffron Hill, London EC1N 8RT, England. Copyright © 1996 Usborne Publishing Ltd. The name Usborne and the device 🎈 are Trade Marks of Usborne Publishing Ltd.

First published in America March 1997.
Printed in Spain.